Unapologetically Here

Naomi P. Washington

Copyright © 2016 Naomi P. Washington

All rights reserved.

Paperback ISBN: 978-0-692-68358-3
EBook ISBN: 978-0-692-68359-0

Published by NewPlaceWithin, LLC.
Cover Design by KLF Design Firm
Edited by Tamika L. Sims, Ink Pen Diva Manuscript Critique Services, LLC

No Portion of this publication may be reproduced, stored in a retrieval system or transmitted in any form by any means electronic, mechanical, photocopying, recording, or any other- except for brief quotations in printed reviews, without the prior written permission of the author.

DEDICATION

Mary Ceonia *"Aunt CeCe"* Davis Albright

You epitomize a life of truth, love, and wisdom. You are forever my blueprint of a woman.

CONTENTS

	Acknowledgments	ii
	Foreword	5
	Introduction	8
Chapter One	Unapologetic by God's Design	11
Chapter Two	I'm Not Perfect	20
Chapter Three	Refereeing Your Own Life	42
Chapter Four	Art of Speaking on Purpose	60
Chapter Five	Stand Up to Stand Out	78
Chapter Six	Make the Choice	91
Chapter Seven	Build Your Support Network	100
	Afterword	105
	About the Author	106

ACKNOWLEDGMENTS

Thank you to the following individuals, without your contributions, this book would not be possible.

Without coaching and methodology, Unapologetically Here, would still be a document on my desktop. Thank you, Ink Pen Diva Manuscript Critique Services, LLC for guiding this book to life. For contributing and mentoring me professionally and personally.

Katrina E. Spigner, thank you for believing in the potential you recognized in me while I sat in your class at Columbia College. I am forever grateful.

Malai Pressley, you and I were introduced on purpose for a purpose. Thank you for your contribution and friendship. Tag you're next!

Thank you: Chris Everett of Chosen One Photography; Kevin Quattlebaum of Personalities Hair Salon; Kristy Quattlebaum Make-Up Artist of Personalities Hair Salon; and, KLF Design Firm for visually wrapping my words with your incredible talent and skills.

I thank the following individuals, who without their support and encouragement this book may not exist.

Thank you to my husband Kevin for listening to the keyboard taps as you tried to sleep and my ramblings as I dreamed out loud until my dreams became a reality. Blessed with three of the most amazing little people this side of Heaven etched in the purest place in my heart. Thank you to my oldest, Sauntavia for sitting up late nights while I wrote and overriding my crazy decisions with, *"Momma, No!"* To my youngest daughter Kearyn, thank you for your positive excitement and always checking in to ask about my writing as a reminder I had deadlines to meet and people waiting. Last but not least, my one and only son Nathan, for standing over my shoulder to read everything out loud as I typed and shared your computer time with me when I interrupted your action hero time.

Thank you to my Mommie, Saundra White, you recited Isaiah 40:30-31 over me until I could believe the scripture myself and I thank you.

"Even youths will become weak and tired, and young men will fall in exhaustion. But those who trust in the Lord will find new strength. They will soar high on wings like eagles. They will run and not grow weary. They will walk and not faint." (Isaiah 40:30–31 New Living Translation, Second Edition)

Blessed with two fathers, I am grateful. To the man who raised me, Charlie Minus thank you for building me and still making me feel like you will always make the world alright.

As referenced later in the book, I acknowledge the memory and love of my Daddy, Virnell Parker. Our relationship has made me the woman I am today.

To my Mother-in-Law and Father-in-Law, Frank and Mary Washington, thank you for always supporting me with encouragement, wisdom, and excitement.

Thank you Ceonia (Cam), Kemberly, Danita, and Sabrina, there is a reason each of you is my sister. You have been a constant source of entertainment and love. No one gets to hug-on me or have me travel more than an hour except you. To my nieces and nephews who I love like my children, thank you for being you.

Cousin, Chaplain Eldred H. Moye Sr, for being the man of God and wisdom. I do not take for granted your willingness to review and as the first reader give feedback on *Unapologetically Here* will. I will always "cherish what more than what is not is."

God made sure I had friends who turned to sisters. Thank you to Christalyn Howard, Charmaine Lewis, Avis Brabham-Moody, Kristian Sanders, Stephanie Henry Payne, Dorian Jeffcoat, Jessica McMillian, Christina Patrick Williams, Tiffany Boykin, Melody Thomas and Anita Ellison-Porter for always pushing me either in writing or my living. No one else gets away with telling me what to do!

Last but not least the young ladies of Young Enchanting Sisters (Y.E.S) and their founders for reminding me I am accountable for my life, and I have goals to achieve.

FOREWORD

With me, what you see is what you get. Yes, call me naive, but I love life. I am happy, and for that, I make no apologies.
~Joyce Geraud

I distinctly remember a time in my life when I consistently used the phrase, "What you see is what you get!" I emphatically claimed that, when you saw me, you were looking at the real thing… Baby! I said it loudly and proudly. I strutted, snapped my fingers, and rolled my neck to drive home the point that I was the real deal! When I stepped away from the audience, and in the stillness of my times alone, there was a startling truth. I was not what everyone saw. I was not the real thing – and the only real deal is, I had become a master of disguise. My loud proclamations were very far from the truth. My life was counterfeit and covered in lies. I was not *thinking*, *speaking*, or *living* my truth – The Truth – God's TRUTH.

Allow me to explain.

When God created each of us, He was intentional. He crafted every intricate detail to His liking and fashioned every fiber of our being according to His plan. God power-packed us with gifts, talents, and abilities. He planned a strategic destiny and charted a specific course for how to get there. He authored our purpose and sealed it in our identity. God chose us before the foundation of the world (Ephesians 1:4).

He chose us to live. God wanted us to love. He chose us to be His authentic creation and to do it without apprehension, without hesitancy, and most importantly, without…. *Apology*.

Merriam-Webster defines *Apology* as, "an expression of regret." In essence, an apology is an acknowledgment we offer when we fail, disappoint, hurt, betray, cause other harm, or even sympathize with others. An apology, in its proper place, can bring comfort, reconciliation, restoration, forgiveness, and trust. However, an apology can be out of place, out of order and just misused. An apology appropriated in the wrong place, well, it could even be deadly.

It becomes deadly when we allow others to cause us to believe we are not enough. It becomes lethal when we tell ourselves we are not enough. It becomes deadly when we become hidden under the multitude of life's layers. The "deadly" part comes in when we choose to live our lives apologetically.

In this book, Naomi Washington uses her own life as a backdrop, as she extends an invitation to you to let go of apologies. On each page, she serves as your guide to delve deeply into understanding God's design for your existence. Naomi walks with you as she helps you face your imperfections with courage and embrace your past with confidence. Through every chapter, Naomi beckons you to stand up and to stand out and to make the choice to live – but not just live – to live UNAPOLOGETICALLY! Get ready for the journey. Your life is about to change.

Katrina Spigner, CPEC, MSW
Founder of Re-Source Solutions, LLC
Author, *Counterfeit: Lies That Cover The Naked Truth*
Columbia, SC

INTRODUCTION

Dear Reader,

Being unapologetic is only one of the many lessons I have learned in my course to authenticity. Much of my life has been an apology. I found myself apologizing for things I did wrong or out of my ignorance. I am by no means confessing perfection on any level at anything. But, in all honesty, I sincerely apologized to keep the peace… and for other reasons. For a long time, I minimized my pursuit of everything God told me He had for me. I spoke and lived beneath my potential to ensure others were never offended. I did not want to appear arrogant in the visions I received for my life. I never tried to set myself apart from others because after all, I made many mistakes. How could I ever be celebrated with a past like mine? How was I going to live the "right" life after living the wrong one for so long?

I learned the first step to reaching my goals and living in my purpose on purpose was to stop counting every moment of excellence as luck and each victory over defeat as chance. I had to become *unapologetic* about my destiny and stop saying, *"I am sorry."* To be sorry means to regret, have pity and sorrow. I was always apologizing to others for following *my* dreams and desires. To apologize meant I felt I had failed or wronged someone. I had to shift my thinking.

I find balance in accepting that for me to be at my best, I must be transparent. I can no longer look for others to use against me the flaws I have because I keep them masked. It is not by accident; you picked up this book. It is not a coincidence you are reading my words. It is time for you to be no longer sorry and apologize for your past. It made us who we are and continued to add value to our lives. Those things are intricate parts of God's design. By God's design, we are connecting at this very moment through words. God has designed your life with and for a purpose. It is your unique plan. You were created inside and out for a purpose, and everything you have gone through or been attacked by was a part of God's design. There are places and positions designed just for you, and no one else can manipulate or imitate your calling for those areas.

Everything that happened in the past did happen. All those things make you who you are and who you will become. Now is the time for you to no longer be sorry and apologize for your past. Be unapologetic about your destiny. Your destiny was charted and choreographed by God long before you were ever conceived. *"For I know the plans I have for you, says the Lord. They are plans for good and not for disaster, to give you a future and a hope (Jeremiah 29: 11 New Living Translation, Second Edition)."* Everything happened and will happen in your life by God's orchestration and plan.

I hope as you turn these pages, you are excited about your destiny and unapologetic about your journey. I hope you identify exactly where you are headed all the while acknowledging where you have been. I pray you find the way to a better you and embrace the experience. This book illustrates my experiences and understanding of living authentically unapologetic. And, wherever you may find yourself in life, I hope that you can proclaim, "I am Unapologetically Here!

"The Lord brought more good to Job in his later years than in his beginning (Job 42:12 New Life Version)."

Forever Striving,

Naomi

CHAPTER ONE
UNAPOLOGETIC BY GOD'S DESIGN

Writing and publishing a book has always been in my heart. The honest truth is while I always wanted to write and publish a book but others reading my thoughts was scary to me. Once upon a time, I was a girl who wrote with no apparent purpose or intent. Writing came natural and in its purest form was cleansing. I wrote to escape. I wrote what I could not speak. Putting pen to paper explained what I could not get others to understand. One day, after years of journaling and expressing myself with words, I went back and read my own words in an old journal. My writing could surmise I had matured.

My automatic response to life as a little girl remained as I grew into a woman with an urge to write. Just as I matured in my writing, so had my desires. The desire to write as a release and escape seasoned into the intentional transparency of my decision to living authentically. I composed sentences with a hope anyone who could identify with them would. I prayed my words would make a connection with anyone needing them. I penned my experiences to share with others. I wrote about the new place I found myself in anticipation of others finding a new place to begin their lives and dreams again.

For you to be holding this book is nothing short of amazing and God's design. I believe this book is all a part of His plan to teach me my writing was never about me. My writing was for someone else and always about Him. When I started this book, I began to understand God's design for me. I examined my life and the lives of those connected to me. I observed the events of our lives and the world around us. I understood all things, good and bad, worked the way they did for a reason. I studied the book of Job in the Bible. In Chapter One of Job, Job is chosen to be tested by Satan with God's permission allowing Satan to take his possessions, but not harm his body, because of his faith. Satan believed Job worshipped God because of the possessions and wealth he was blessed. Through the tests, Job continues in faith never cursing God. Satan then goes back to God and is granted permission to do as he pleases to Job, but spare his life.

In my life, there have been many tests orchestrated by God. Tests, He permitted. I do not believe we go through any trial or struggle without God's approval. Through everything, I came out with my life spared. Just like Job, I lost some family and friends. There were times my money was short, and my possessions were few. My body was under attack, and there were moments when I should have lost my mind. There were moments I was on the verge of a nervous breakdown as a part of God's design.

My unapologetic journey has been arduous, and for only one reason, please allow me one moment to go ahead and be transparent for us to move on. Writing to you is safer for me than standing in front of you. I was consistently in my way. I committed to memory every negative thing ever said to or about me. I was not qualified to stand up in a room and motivate others. I believed every word ever said to me, about me. If I thought it, I knew you would as well. My safe, comforting place was and has always been to write. Here is my routine, I sit down at the computer, open a new document and begin to write. Sometimes, I have a purpose and other times I need to satisfy my insatiable urge to get thoughts on paper.

However, there are periods in my life when I would, more often than not, bypass my computer altogether. I did not grab my phone to focus on typing in my publication app. I did not send myself an e-mail of reflections nor did I send to my cell number a series of texts from my thoughts. I ignored the need to write altogether. During one of my hiatus' from writing, during Christmas 2015, my son walked up to me and said, *"Mom, why don't you blog anymore?"* I said, *"I am busy."*

The truth is, I was not busy. I was out of focus. I found every excuse available to do everything except the very thing I needed to do. My sabbatical had more to do with me knowing what I needed to do, but not wanting to. Those moments when I break from writing are so much more profound than just writing. During the hiatus of 2015, I had not been writing because I had not wanted to come to terms with the familiarity of writing. For me, the familiarity of words flowing calmed my spirit and confronted my fears. The writing was my safe place for clarity's sake. It meant if I sat down to write for my self-awareness, words would either become my conviction of inadequacy or my affirmation of accomplishment. I was not even in a position to confront myself. Writing clears my thoughts as I seek to understand and comprehend. I had a conversation with my writing coach and shared my struggles when I began the process of writing this book. She said I needed to stop being "safe." I had never written what needed to be said, but rather what I felt others wanted or needed to hear. So, writing when I was not ready to come to terms with my own life was just a disaster waiting to happen.

My decision to grow and be 'unapologetically here' lead me to ask myself some hard questions when I sat down to write. If I write about how my decisions haunt me enough to cry more often than I anticipated or how mean girls turn into mean women, what would people think? If I was honest about missing my father who died when I was 27 and apologized for his alcoholism and absence only months before his demise would those closest to him be upset with my revelation? Should I be honest about the confusion in my heart for wanting more than anything to relieve the aching in my soul by just hearing him one more time say how much he loved me? Just because his "I love you" was the truest and most familiar love I ever knew. Would this be too much for others to hear? Apologizing when I was hurt was easier than letting the hurt go. So I apologized. When I say I spent so much of my life apologizing, I do not mean my articulation of, "I am sorry" or "I apologize."

I apologize for meetings when I do not speak as a means to not upset those around me. I apologize for my dress when I feel the need to try harder as a plus size female. I apologize for compromising my decisions to appease those around me on a daily basis. While I tread lightly to make no intentional or indirect offense to others, I tell my purpose, *"I am sorry."* I tell everything God used to mold, shape, and position the design of who I am, *"I apologize, they're not ready for you."*

My husband once told me I had a pattern in my writing to focus on cutting people out of my life. He called me to the carpet. My approach to dealing with situations was for anything needing to be confronted to cut away. Was this the message I wanted to convey? In my attempt to empower with my writing. I was telling readers to push others away. I was providing tips from my toolbox. Writing or speaking to others was more comfortable if I cut everyone who hurt me out of my life. Cutting people out of my life is so much cleaner than confronting the issues, growing in the conflict and acknowledging my worth. I chose to sugar coat my writing. I did not write or say anything impolite or politically incorrect. Newsflash! I sugar coated all the things needing to be told and deleted entire sentences to make what others wanted to hear my priority.

Finally, I reveal my truth. Deep breath. I am flawed. We all are. I believed deep down if I apologized enough, said and did what kept everyone happy then my life would somehow be of worth. If I were able to live and move forward masking my flaws, they would somehow disappear. Then I stopped writing. I became the helpless helper and the motivator who lacked assurance while encouraging others on a daily basis. While I was inspiring others to live their greatness I couldn't see my own. I didn't like the place I was in and felt writing would only force a conversation on paper with my flaws and insecurities. As I looked into my son's beautiful eyes when he asked why I was not writing, I knew God was giving me the permission I felt it wasn't ok to give myself. In my effort to become authentic and transparent to others, I first had to be confrontational and authentic with myself. It was my unapologetic personal assault. After some hard conversations and moments sitting in who I had become, I realized I was sorry. I owed myself a genuine apology. I cheated myself out of everything God promised me. I was living up to the expectation of others while drifting further away from the purpose He designed for me. I took a step back one day and had to ask myself a question. *"Why do I have to apologize for being who I am?"* How authentically am I living out my purpose by playing everything safe and apologizing for someone else's discomfort with the truth? Sometimes it wasn't even a truth they had control over because it was my own. I apologized. I tried living my life being all things to all people before and it almost killed me.

For a long time, I considered myself to be superwoman. I was able to work a full-time demanding job and take care of my family. Playing the roles and being the person I needed to be for everyone around me. The entire time, I felt as if I was juggling all the other demands of life in stride. I was able to meet deadlines with swiftness, while taking on anything coming at me unexpectedly and managed to do it all effortlessly. Little did I know, on the inside, my mind and body were screaming for me to stop. They were calling out to me with modest aches and pains here and there I graciously smiled away. I continued to put myself further down my list of priorities.

I was able to balance everything on one small plate and ever so slightly push the needed component of Naomi away. I was forgetting the relevant part of spending time with me. I never let myself breathe from one thing to the next. There were many demands placed on my life, but I never commanded the attention I deserved. Then it hit me – abruptly. April 14, 2009, I felt a pounding in my head as if a little man knocking on the inside trying to get out. My stress and struggle were beginning to manifest itself in my body unexpectedly. The events of the next six months taught me many things about myself and the decisions for the rest of my life. To put it plainly, I was able to process in the six months after that day what was important, I was neglecting to breathe, and superwoman was choking the life out of me.

My unapologetic presence in my own life became crucial after the apology I made to myself; I became unapologetic about my life and the person I had become as a result. I had to grow unapologetic about my destiny and stop saying, *"I am sorry."*

There are things we should apologize for and things we shouldn't. We should never apologize for becoming better, making necessary changes or reaching for more significant than our current state of existence. We should never fall into a place of apologizing for following dreams and accomplishing goals. We should dismiss the urge to apologize for our dedication, excellence, and advancement. We do. Essentially, we are apologizing for our destiny.

Every event, no matter how large or small happens for a reason. Every moment, all the decisions and every action are catalysts to your destiny. My life has taught me to look at things as only a part of my journey. Situations and circumstances have only been brief stops on my itinerary. They have been temporarily a part of my life, but never my final destination. I had to shift my thinking to treat them as such. It became essential to separate every position for my purpose.

It is time for me to package the lessons in my heart between these two covers. Time to pass along the lessons I learned when there were words, my heart could not say. It is necessary to release the lessons I learned when I had eyes that would not stop crying and a voice that was silenced by hurt for my growth.

Yes, I've made plenty of mistakes, but in the end, there is no one else I would rather be than me. I have gone from the little girl with her words scribbled in a journal into a woman hoping her words bound in a cover would guide someone on their life's journey. The little girl in me is excited this book has come to fruition, and the woman in me is elated you hold them in your hand.

CHAPTER TWO
I'M NOT PERFECT

I have become accustomed to the unusual guesses about what my middle name. No one ever guesses my maiden name, which is Parker. The most common beliefs are Patricia, Patrice and Penelope, yes, Penelope. While the game of guessing what my middle initial means gets interesting, the conclusions people make about my life are even more interesting. What I can tell you is they would never look at me and guess at random the "P" at one point represented pregnancy. If they knew my story, they wouldn't say it stood for perfect either. Perfect and pregnant are the two words which changed my life. These two "p" words would begin shaping me into the woman I am today. While I have never been a perfect person, becoming pregnant at 15 was a sure way of declaring it to everyone else. I still remember the words coming from my lips in a whisper with my head bowed, *"Mommy, I'm pregnant."*

The words came out in a shiver when I was 15 in the tenth grade. My older sister, Kem stood there with me. She told my mother for me. My mother, a strong woman, committed to teaching her four daughters to be responsible and accountable, required me to say it to her in my voice. She wanted to hear it from me, not a spokesperson. What was said, I don't remember after those three words. I eventually went back to my bedroom. I remember the walk taking longer than it did any other time in my life. My bedroom was a retreat away from everything else in our home. Lying in bed, I knew what I felt in my belly was not nervous butterflies, but for a few seconds, I knew it should have been.

I don't remember if the television was on or music was playing. I don't recall a phone ringing or anyone speaking. I stared at the popcorn ceiling for what seemed like a lifetime. The light from my bedside lamp illuminated the wall cascading a shadow to the spot where I focused. Then I felt it. There it was, a kick. As tears filled my ears after six months of holding the broken pieces of my life and my breath, I finally released a deep sigh.

I was a sophomore in high school. I quit marching band in July when camp started and decided I was going to do something different. I never intended for my different to be pregnant. Sure enough, I was. My older sisters, Kem and Cam, lived in Atlanta. Kem had been getting phone calls from friends and other people telling her I was pregnant. President's Day weekend of February 1998, she came home to South Carolina and slept in the bed with me. I am very particular about my personal space, so Kem sharing my room and bed with me for her impromptu visit was very uncomfortable. My area, already occupied, resulted in me being more nervous than usual and I didn't want to run the risk of her knowing.

We talked, and I denied the whole time of her creative interrogation I was having a baby. However, I already felt the baby move and kick for the first time on my birthday in December. We went to Wal-Mart for a pregnancy test. We came back home, and she stood there in the bathroom with me. Do not get me wrong, I looked, walked and felt pregnant. In my 16-year-old mind, if it looked pregnant, walked pregnantly and felt pregnant, you guessed it. I just wasn't going to admit it to Kem. So I took the pregnancy test. I went along with the "question and answer" game all the way up until the test confirmed what I already knew, she suspected, and we now needed to tell my mother.

I was pregnant with no plan. I did not have a sincere desire for my life yet. Remember, I was 16 in the second semester of my sophomore year. I was not planning anything for my future at the time in my life this was all taking place. I had no plan with a baby in it. I remember the emotional pain in the days to follow. I felt supported but had let so many people down. My mother was quiet for a very long time. She supported me in every way needed, making sure to care for my daughter and I once she arrived. I did not know the strength she had then, but as a mother, I see now.

She stood tall, faced gossip and things I was completely unaware of until reaching adulthood, which at the time as a naïve 16-year-old would not have been prepared to handle. My step-father, Charlie did not say much. Not that I believe he would have, but he knew fussing or chastising me was not an option. Through the remaining 4 months of my pregnancy after me telling them, Charlie would make sure I ate and laughed to lighten my spirits. If he could have put me in a bubble to isolate me from the world and all I was enduring at the time, I believe he would have. My biological father, Virnell cried. He expressed to me how disappointed he was with me. I remember thinking, *"Why?"* I was the one pregnant and 16, why did he need to be consoled? I completely dismissed his disappointment because, in my thoughts, I cannot let down someone who never set me up to be anything better than what I already was.

My world was not perfect, but I felt I lived up to everything others said I would be at the very moment I said those three words to my mother… nothing. What chances did I have raising a baby and being successful? What opportunities would I have to go to college? How much of a burden to my family was I going to be with a baby? No, "P" does not stand for Patricia or Penelope. It does not initial possibilities, potential or promise either. It does not stand for perfect. What does the word "perfect" mean anyway?

I like to perform word autopsies. It is so crucial for me to know what a word means when I use it. According to *Merriam-Webster,* "perfect" is defined as having all the required or desirable elements, qualities, or characteristics and being as good as it is possible to be. Wow! Society has trained us to believe by definition, perfect, is attainable. We were convinced perfection exists. We are all in search at some point in our lives for "perfect." We believe there is a perfect spouse, car, home or career to meet our desires. How does perfect look? If we search the aisle in the grocery store, we find magazine covers filled with perfection. The perfect couple, people and body, all graphically designed right there, from the magazine to magazine. We have such a short attention span in our world until perfection is limited to what holds us as a captive audience for the moment. We are striving for perfection in everything and becoming good at nothing. I say "we" because we have all been there. I travel down that road often when I decide to bake.

I love Pinterest, and it makes me believe I can do whatever I want in my kitchen. I love baking. I am not sure if I love eating or baking. For this book, we will say I love baking. I peruse Pinterest and Google to find recipes all the time. More often than not, I become intrigued by the photos of pastry delights. I quickly make a list of things needed and head to the store. I may purchase the "store brand" or sale item to save money. I use the list of what is needed and the recipe itself. I glance at the photo to double check my items and head to make my purchases with excitement. In delight and anticipation, once I arrive home, I begin the process of following measurements and directions to create the photo I keep referencing on my handheld device.

Sometimes I achieve a level of satisfaction with my finished product, and there are times I miss the mark - by a significant and substantial miss. There was one cheesecake concoction that could have probably been a science fair experiment. I have never reached perfection with anything I baked or cooked. No matter how many recipes I try or what I call my specialty in the kitchen, nothing ever comes out the same as the last time. There are no "Voila!" moments either. I made some lemon bars once mistaken for cornbread by my brother in law Jermaine. I don't think he has eaten anything else I cooked since then.

The strive for perfection is no different than my cornbread lemon squares. Perfection varies from person to person; these variations based on preference. It is why we should be careful when we strive for the lifestyles and standards of others. The perfect vacation for me is home in my bed asleep. For someone with no children and the demands I have in my life, an ideal vacation could be crystal blue water beaches and glasses with umbrellas.

We are carrying the standards of perfection passed down to us. Some of us are striving to make everyone else proud. We are diligently focusing on not embarrassing our parents or families for the sake of a standard. We imitate parenting styles of our parents because we don't want to let them down when we raise our own. Living up to the labels from small towns and academic success from high school, we enter into career fields trying so hard to excel and later feel trapped or stifled. I had an interesting conversation with a friend once who worked in her corporate career field in a big city.

Her mother was very proud of her for obtaining her graduate degree, but how she illustrated her feelings for me was a description of being shackled by the chains of perfection. She said she felt her creativity ooze out her ears in a business meeting one day. She was reading a proposal and began crying from the agony of just wanting to paint and create colorful illustrations of life on a canvas. She was so busy chasing the dreams of her mother until she had not picked up a paintbrush in three years. It was like a piece of her soul was packed away because it was not acceptable.

We hold on to failed marriages to keep up the

appearances of families modeled in car commercials or church fans. The images are smiling back at us growing up. You know the family I am referencing. The one dressed in their Easter Sunday outfit in front of the stain glassed window or the one all churches seem to be using on their websites? The family is sitting in front of a home, with their two children laughing and the sun is shining. I have seen it at banks as well. There is nothing like a perfect family who attends church and has good credit, right? My great aunt and uncle gave me some valuable information when I got married. *"Do not take marriage advice from anyone not married or who are divorced."* Marriage is not perfect; it is personal. However, are we not merely striving to make everything perfect because nothing is private anymore? What is holding you captive from your purpose? What is the perfection you strive for in your life? Is it realistic?

When I had my daughter at 16, my aunt and uncle cared for me while on homebound from school before her delivery and then afterward. While they were in their late 60's and retired, they were able to care for us while my mother worked. My aunt took me to the prenatal doctor visit. On the way back home after an appointment, she stopped beside the road. I thought something was wrong. Now, my Aunt CeCe is a little short, energetic, fast-talking woman of wisdom. Before I could even figure out what she was doing, she hopped back in my Uncle Jim's Buick, cranked up and shifted into drive. We were back on the road.

Beside her in the seat lay the purple flowers she plucked from the shoulder of the road. Yep, "P" stands for purple, purpose, and pretty. Those purple flowers on the side of a back road from Orangeburg to Blackville in South Carolina caught her eye as she drove a 16-year-old pregnant teenager back home from the doctor. Who plucks flowers from the side of the road? Aunt CeCe finds beauty and perfection in the imperfection of things. Is that not what God is asking of us? Even in the messiness of the situation, she saw beauty beside the road. Sometimes, we need reminding of the beauty of our imperfections.

The pictures and images of perfection are suffocating us as models and holy grails. In truth, while striving to reach perfection, we let go of the reality of living. In the pursuit, we neglect to recognize moments in life presented as opportunities, allowing and positioning us to become who God designed us to be before created. Unapologetic thinking establishes a principle to abandon all our thoughts of perfection.

Accept an understanding of your journey that things will not be perfect all the time. There are going to be some hard moments. There will be times when everything will go right, and you will experience close illusions of perfection. Then, there are going to be moments you will question everything. I have been there in those moments myself. I have questioned everything in my life down to the paint color on my bathroom wall. It is mint green by the way. I've had many moments of being in doubt running from agony to pain over decisions in my life. While looking at the lives of others, we see their celebration. How often do we take the vantage point of seeing their celebration and not the work they applied to their achievement? Or even compare the accomplishment to the work we are putting into our own lives?

If you missed the point of anything written before this, I want to make sure you understand perfection does not exist. Your designed destiny is not going to be mapped out correctly. Your life may very well have more hard places than easy ones. I encourage you to know it is all worth it. Think unapologetically about the status of your life, goals, and dreams. Think with no reservations to anyone other than yourself. Unapologetically seizing opportunities leads to the discovery of passions hidden within your heart. Prepare and position yourself for great things. In case you didn't know, God does not need your help. He does not need permission from those around you or assistance from anyone else to provide the blessings He has for you. God knows what He is doing. He blesses better than I bake. He will not miss the mark for anything He does. You will make mistakes, and it is ok. Sometimes the beauty in mistakes is the provision they allow for us to do better. I learned from errors when I was ten years old in the fourth grade.

As a child, I was quiet. Most times I could be found reading. I began reading *The State Newspaper* when I was in the first grade. There was something different for me when I read the newspaper. I read anything I could get my hands on, but every day I was drawn to find something in the newspaper. My mother was a daily subscriber for many years. I remember reading and cutting out articles to read over and over again. I learned about Desert Storm every chance I could. I preferred reading over watching the television. I was amazed by the articles of the Berlin Wall destroyed in 1990. When my Uncle told me he had been to Germany, I was amazed. When I became older, I read about the South Carolina controversy over the Confederate Flag, missing children and other events in the Metro section. Although I read so many things, I did not understand many of them as I do now.

I was consumed by what I read and would escape to another place. I felt I was a part of something bigger than what was going on around me. I was able to avoid the teasing from peers in the classroom, which resulted in me shutting down to my surroundings. When I shut down, I lost an understanding of my academics. I was moved from the "A section" in the 4th grade to the "B section" in the 5th grade. I do not believe they still classify students this way, but when I moved down it was horrible. The classification by academic standing of students in a rural South Carolina school was essentially a modern form of segregation. My 4th-grade year was challenging. Math was not my favorite subject and my math teacher, who shall remain nameless, played a game called "Around the World." We would take turns going to the board doing math problems. If you got the problem right, you stayed on the board for the next round with another student. If you missed it, then you would sit down. The goal was to have one student left standing in an attempt to present the winner. Looking back, I am not sure if this was the correct way to go about establishing academic achievement with nine and ten years old in front of their peers. Well, you may as well have asked me to go up in front of the room and speak German. I was terrified and struck out every time.

    I would walk to the board, my back turned to the other students and stared at it. I was frozen. Then there was the day that changed my little ten-year-old life. This particular day, after standing at the board for a while, she sent me back to my seat. I guess she had enough because as I walked back to my seat, the mistake of not completing the problem sent her into a rant. My mistake made her angry. At that moment, while I walked back to my seat, she called me stupid in front of the entire class. All I could do was sink in my seat. While the game continued with the next students and the "mean girls" snickering, I died inside. It was the moment when a mistake had seemingly become the end of my ten-year-old world.

There was no newspaper to read in escape from reality. I could only look down at my math book. At the end of the school day, I went home and told my mother, who was a teacher in another school district. My mother and I both fell silent. There was a difference in the silence. Mine was a silence of retreat, and my mothers was a slow simmer. If liquids simmer long enough, they begin to boil. Once I let my mother know about the incident, I went on with my evening doing what I usually did, read. The next morning, as my sister and I were getting ready for school, my mother prepared for work. Only today, something appeared to be different. She did not take us to Big Mama's house to walk to school; she took us *to* school. She said nothing. My sister said nothing. We both knew she was going to school with one of us. We just stared at one another.

I was sure the regular routine of being in a classroom with a ranting math teacher was the nature of fourth grade. After all, I was the one who made a mistake. I did not complete the problem, and she got angry. I was stupid, right? I knew the math problems. I was in the class. I was the one not able to do it. It was a mistake on my part because when I was in Ms. Pigman's third-grade class, I loved her math lessons. It was me, math and Around the World game. It was my fault, but how could I tell my mother this from the back seat. No need to ask my sister Sabrina to say anything to her. She wasn't going to be my voice either. She is my mother's mini. She may be my little sister, but there were times she stood up for me when I couldn't stand up myself. I just needed my mother to know why it was all my fault. I did not focus in class or pay attention and do my work, so that was why I was terrible at "Around the World." I was not as smart as the other kids. I wished I could get her attention to tell her I was stupid. I was just stupid when it came to math. While I went to homeroom, my mother went to meet with my math teacher. 4th-grade math changed for me that day.

I made a mistake in math that day just the same way I make mistakes in life now. While I was upset over my mistake as a ten-year-old and justifying the actions of others because of my error, my mother was interceding on my behalf. She had done this before. In first grade, our teacher would slap our knuckles if we did not bring in homework or talked in class. My first-grade teacher slapped everyone's knuckles except one student for talking in class. It was when my mother interceded, and I was able to understand her actions for the very first time.

This time reminded me of first grade. Just as in first grade, my mother called another parent to see if they knew what happened. She weighed her options as it pertained to responding. In each incident, she came to the school the next morning. She stood in the folds for me. She advocated on my behalf, but I made a mistake. Was I talking in first grade? Honestly, I probably wasn't, but who can remember. I missed the math problem. At ten, I did not think my teacher was wrong to call me stupid because she was the teacher. If she said I was stupid, I was stupid. Then I grew up.

Many more times I would make a mistake and let it define me. With every mistake, I built a wall of defense, read and escaped. The most unfortunate part of making a mistake is they were all my perception. The mistake of telling a lie. The error of being in the wrong place, at the wrong time, doing what I was not supposed to be doing was who Naomi was. As in math, I made careless mistakes and sometimes I never bounced back from them. Being unapologetic is about resiliency. It is about being able to make a mistake and be ok with having made one. I had to accept while I made mistakes, I had to take ownership of the learning process as well. Every mistake made, required me to get back up, dust myself off and keep moving. I could not shut down.

I grew up and reading the paper did not work

as much for me as an adult as it had when I was a child. Purpose and authenticity require growth and progression. Sometimes the lessons from the mistakes are what propel you toward your purpose. It is all necessary for your destiny. For a baby to learn to walk, they must first fall. With a baby learning to walk, others intercede on their behalf, the mistakes made in the beginning are not the mistakes continued in the process. However, the process of growth is like walking, and some of us are clumsier than others needing support from time to time.

There was importance in knowing and understanding where I was in life. I cannot accept who I will become if I continue to operate in who I was. Yes, I needed to do better! Focusing and rationalizing your mistakes will have you respond from an apologetic posture. We base our responses to situations on our current positions in life. Deep down I expected my mother to come to school when I told her what happened. I will be the first to admit even as an adult; my mother is my bodyguard when someone has hurt me or if I need her.

However, in the event I am wrong, all bodyguard responsibilities are null and void. She corrects me. I can be authentic because I have a compass to understand my genuine mistakes and when I am coming from an ugly place. We all have moments when we do things and in the name of ignorance, pretend we did not know any better. Yes, those moments. Stop it! Unapologetically humble yourself and apologize when you are wrong and even ignorant.

Unapologetically, I have made mistakes, and I am ok with that. It was essential in my quest for authenticity for me to come out of the books and abandon the escape plan when I did. I decided to stop allowing my mistakes to shut down my voice. I was giving up on myself at every turn in some things. I was sure as an adult my flaws were my barrier. Girls like me who have babies as teens do not mentor others. Children like me who grow without the brands and labels do not deserve them as adults. No one handed me anything as a teen mom, and I believe for nothing to be as an adult. No freebies. Growing up, I thought I was not deserving of anything good. That is the way I felt. It was the reality I felt in myself.

I had to destroy the position and condition of things in my life. My status quo was not helping anyone around me. It was keeping me unhappy with everything. I was not having conversations with people who were important to me because I knew it meant relationships would shift. I felt I was not deserving of love so who was I to define how I wanted to be loved or what I would even accept? How could I tell someone I no longer wanted them in my life when I was no better than they were? I was complacent with the discomfort of misunderstandings because getting to the heart of the matter meant there could be hurtful truths. My status quo may be different from yours. We sabotage the progress to our purpose with behaviors from issues in our past. We are not moving forward because we are fearful of past mistakes and doubts. We are continuing to hold ideas and squash dreams because of ties to seasonal people and positions we somehow made permanent due to complacency.

Let's admit it; we are comfortable with the current position of our lives because it is safe. The way my life is set up, I cannot be stagnant. I know I will never reach my highest potential if I do not grow every day. On the days I am not building in my career, I know I need to look for opportunities to advance. I look for webinars or articles on the latest theory or social issue calling for action. I have to destroy the status quo of being complacent.

We are afraid to step out into our dream of owning businesses, going back to school or even having courageous conversations about what we want from relationships. For some people, the status quo is as simple as not calling the loved one we wronged because an apology would mean the healing process must begin. For you to be the person you are destined to, you must acknowledge your current state of affairs. In your life at this moment, what is the current state of your affairs?

Unapologetic thinking is to change the way you think about things thoroughly. For a long time, I felt misunderstood. Due to feeling misunderstood, I stopped trying to *be* understood. I was consumed with the notion of no one understanding what I was saying or feeling. I was frustrated. I would go into my shut down mode. Not only would I shut down but I would cut people entirely off and out of my life. I doubted myself and became discouraged about everything. Then it dawned on me; I wasn't communicating what I needed them to know. I wasn't saying I needed support. I didn't tell them I needed them to love and encourage me. If I had stayed in this place in my life, you wouldn't be reading this book. I had to change the existing state of my affairs by doing something different.

A few years ago, while washing dishes, I noticed the picture frames on my living room wall were crooked. They had been for weeks, maybe even months. The photos represented all the things important in my life, family, love, and growth. They were crooked. I never determined if the wall shifted, the photos put up crooked or if some object hit them! At the time my son was about three years old, so flying toy cars, balls and other miscellaneous objects in our household was very common. While in the middle of washing a plate I decided, *"OK, time to move!"*

I was no longer going to stand there and look at the photos on the wall in their current crooked position. I had to take my hands off of the dishes. I had to relinquish my focus on what I was doing and change the current position of my frames. I went into the garage, grabbed the "bubble level thingy," and did it. I went into the sacred domain of my husband, the garage, and got additional equipment. I moved the furniture and knocked a few things over, but after some adjustment, done! All this time, my pictures didn't change, fall or even have a distorted image. Only the frames were crooked! The frames, which held my photographs shifted and moved. Not my love, life and growth, just the frames!

Shifting to your purpose is just like moving frames. The principles, values, and beliefs we have are frames holding us together. Your purpose shows up in everything you do. You can fight it, hide it and run from it, but it shows up. Regardless of what our mothers planned for us, the timeline of events, we must achieve to be happy or even the understanding of specific material items giving us special statuses to others. Your purpose is your purpose. If you are driving a $5,000 or a $50,000 car, what God has designed for your life will come to fruition.

When you don't operate in your life with this new understanding, you could produce the same results you have in the past. If we are not ready to shift some things around in our thinking about life, relationships, money, faith and people we will forever be in the same crooked position we have always been.

Just like my wall photos, we sometimes have to move a few things to make the frame straight. Find a way to pull it all together, move, push and even destroy some things in your way. It may require some extra work. It may require you to take a few classes, read a few books and attend a few conferences. It may need you to stop talking to people stuck in the same financial rut as you. It may require you to connect with couples who have been married 50 years as opposed to spending time, the ones who are not married or married the same amount of time as you. Sometimes the best way to understand life is to understand it through the path of someone who has experienced it.

It endorses your understanding of your current situation is temporary. You don't have to stay in the same place you are at this very moment. The very thing you are going through is preparing you for what God purposed you to do. While in your current situation, remember, there is another side to where you. It would be very similar to the preparation for running a race. The best way to learn about the marathon for this year is to talk with someone who ran last year. In some situations, you may be fortunate enough to speak with the person who won. You have to become determined to move. You have to be ok with changing your way of thinking, learning new things, and being open to understanding new things. Decide to shift your thinking about your current state of affairs. Things will at times feel uncomfortable, unfamiliar and even be scarier than you would like to admit. Know God can keep up with it all. It is all in His hands, in His time and His plans.

To make your life shift and dreams come true, you have to abandon the status quo. Shake up all those things around you which have become stagnant and complacent. Growing and shifting require some things to be out of place. It's important to remember; it's only temporary. You can no longer stand in your current situation and expect different results. It is time to picture yourself exactly where you want to be in life. Make a conscious effort and action to recreate the very things you envision for your life. It is time to destroy your current situation, shift the existing state of affairs and walk into your destiny. No more standing still. Not one of us is perfect, but we don't have to neglect the strive for excellence. Unapologetically, I strive after every mistake, before every decision, and in every situation to be who God has called me to be. Will you?

CHAPTER THREE
REFEREEING YOUR OWN LIFE

My husband is a football fan. I prefer basketball, but several years ago, I realized I had no choice but to learn and understand the language of football to communicate with him from August to February. The South Carolina Gamecocks and Pittsburgh Steelers dominate our home on Thursday, Saturday, Sunday, and Monday. If either of those teams is not playing, he still watches to see what other teams are doing. As I began to learn the art of the gridiron, I realized a few years ago life was really like football.

As I began finding and acknowledging my purpose, I realized I had been playing all the positions on the field at different times in my life. Sometimes I was the quarterback, making moves and looking for the best person to carry the ball all the way to the end zone. There were days I needed to be the middle linebacker and tackle opponents carrying things I did not want to manifest or score in my life. In my position as a running back, I was always determined to carry out my purpose the offensive linemen on my team, opened and made holes for me.

One position I always play for myself without fail is a referee. My stepfather, Charlie, and my Uncle Jim were baseball umpires when I was growing up.

When on the field they looked like different people. Not because of their uniform, but because of the attention, precise and exact movements they made to capture every part of the field. Nothing could break their attention. No cheering, yells, coaches, players warming up or sand flying around at times. Their attention was focused. Finding your purpose and unapologetically living it entails you referring your life.

My stepfather, Charlie was a baseball player. He had not always been the referee. So his referee perspective on the game was one of player depth and regulation knowledge. It made sense for him to transition into the role of umpire when you think about it. After many years of playing the game, he had the advantage to call the games in a fair and regulated manner. Referees have the same goal no matter the sport. A referee is an official person who watches the game carefully to monitor rules and arbitrate the issues arising during the plays. The same objective is needed when you referee your own life.

Football is ugly, tiring and messy. As a mother, I don't look forward to the day my son decides he wants to play football. Football is a sport where injuries are more likely to happen. Much like life, it is not a field of dreams. You have to work and make every effort to enter the end zone. Making plays is harder with some opponents than others. In basketball, you make the shot, get a chance to rebound and retake it. In football, it's not that easy. If you fumble, the opponent's recovery could win the game with their possession.

When I first began watching football with my husband, Ray Lewis was scary to me. I would stop in my tracks if he were on television. His intensity was terrifying and overwhelming. Then when he got on the field, it was terrific. The man was like a Pitbull. He charged fast and fierce to stop any momentum the other team planned to make. Whew! I need a minute just thinking about how he played. Life has its similarities to football. We are facing rivalries to our purpose with just as much intensity as teams playing Ray Lewis and the Baltimore Ravens. My most prominent competition to purpose was my past. My past was standing there staring at me square in the face. It was like Ray Lewis.

When our past recovers our fumbles, it hurts. The opposing team and their fans take record of it. Never letting us live one fumble down. The opposition celebrates knowing yet again we have been defeated from winning in life towards our purpose. I believe the devil attacks us because he knows when we are getting close to what God has planned for us. Some people in your life will keep a record of every bad play and penalty which pushes the chains further away from the goal line.

Remember, I said Ray Lewis scared me? The reason is Ray Lewis reminded me of a pit bull. I am terrified of dogs. I never had a reason to dislike dogs. I have always been afraid of dogs, but when I was 33, I was bitten by one. My fear of dogs is from childhood. Everyone close to me knows my fear of dogs. It's clear to my grandmother and others their dogs need to be put outside, on short leashes or in other rooms when I visit. It's a requirement. Much like my fear of dogs defines the scope of how who and when I will visit a person's home, such as how our past defines us.

My grandmother loves dogs, and I love my Grandma Mildred. So, of course, I am vigilant of her dog, GiGi during my visits. She has to put GiGi out of the house when I come to visit. I come in the front door and GiGi goes out the back one. We have a system, and it works. Unfortunately, as we navigate to becoming unapologetic, we have defined the scope of our existence by our past. We strategize our game plans based on the extent of our history while the opposition develops a plan for us on what it has defined us to be. I learned to use my past as an influence and not as the definition of who I am. I am using my past, but for you, it could very well be something else. Hurt, fear, shame or insecurities can define how we operate in our purpose.

All those things operate in teams of opposition.

Organizations would create offensive plays around Ray Lewis. They had to get around his intensity. He had a reputation for being a leader and intimidating as a middle linebacker. He led his team in tackles for 12 of his 14 seasons. The team did not allow a single 100-yard rusher for 51 consecutive games from 1998 through 2001 seasons. Other teams had to come up with strategies before the game to make sure he did not "get in their head." If he was not running over you, he was talking to you. His pregame banter was intense as well. He is the true definition of "Turn-Up." The man was sweating out of the tunnel! While this was his real and genuine form of play, it had also to prove overwhelming to opponents. Especially those who had never experienced him. Teams prepared for games with him based on his behaviors, record, and level of play. The Baltimore Ravens defense was successful because Ray Lewis made sure everyone in his line moved with the same plan of stopping the other team from scoring. While Ray Lewis influenced the methods and strategies of teams, it was never who he was as a man.

As I learned more about Ray Lewis, I realized his greatness and passion on the field was only a part of who he was as a man. The intensity seen on the field is his pursuit of living out his God-designed purpose. Through foundations, philanthropic and faith, he has defined himself off the field. Despite some negativity in the public eye, he never wavered in his purpose-on or off the field. His past only influenced the man he has become. While the opposition of our history is always present, we have to move forward still.

While others choose to build perceptions and opinions based on my past, I have the power to boldly execute my plans to define who I am walking into my purpose. You have that same ability in your life as well with faith over fear, success over shame and independence in spite of insecurities. We control how we move forward in life when we choose to win. We can referee our game and set the rule over the opposition. Never allowing defeat to be an option.

I decided to accept responsibility for what happens beyond this point in life. I am responsible for moving my purpose forward. I have to move the chains. It requires some changing and decisions. As we look our opponents in the eye and hear their fans cheering them on to stop our momentum towards purpose, we have to choose. Choose whether you win or lose at this point. The places you use to go, people you associated with, things you are and are not proud of in your past, the fans are waving in front of you on banners and reminding you they have defeated you before.

Between you and the end zone of purpose is the matter of fact idea you will "get-what-you-deserve" and "what happened to you was because of a decision you made." You let that idea grab your last interception of opportunity. Now the idea has become your belief affecting how you play the rest of this game. As a direct result of your past, you clear your sideline and roster of people who try to love you or get close and build with you. While you are re-structuring your team, the oppositions of your past hurt and anger are continuing to line up against you, ready. When you are strategizing with every ounce of energy and focus on your past, you lose the opportunity to condition the present for the strength needed in the future. Recognize when you dwelled in pity over what you don't have and missed out on you forget everything you do have in your present moment. Sometimes we hold on to the past because it is familiar then replay one game over and over again. It is comfortable to stay right at the moment rather than move on to prepare for the next.

That is what happened during a critical part of my life. It was the game I played against my father. Cancer controlled the game clock. I found comfort for many quarters, allowing anger and disappointment to coach from the sidelines while embarrassment and fear cheered loudly from my stands. I developed strategy plays focusing on the man I was comfortable believing he was. A person's way strong wat of thinking impacts their decision to change. People can change. If there is one thing you can always count on about others, it's they have a past. Everyone has a past directly influencing their ability and decision to change. Some people have a hard time accepting the past of others' and the ability to change. This book is not about how we deal with people in their ability to change it is about our ability to adapt. For me, my past was the most prominent opponent hindering me from walking into my purpose.

My father was an alcoholic. I held on to every memory of seeing him drunk when he did not know I saw him. I held on to every hurt, I remember from hearing him yell in his inebriation when I was younger than five. I remember all the embarrassing times going to NAACP Youth Council meetings and him watching drunk at the corner store. I will never forget how uncomfortable it was to see his name in the county paper after his arrest criminal domestic violence or non-payment of child support.

All those memories were blocking me from gaining an understanding of the man he was. I remember being on the phone with him sometime in 2008. It was several months after I had my son. We argued, and it was terrible. I said some things, he said some things, and he hung up on me. I called back to ask, "Did you just hang up on me?". I was heartbroken. I would never challenge or dispute his love for me. I knew without a shadow of a doubt he loved me. I would never disrespect him because he was my father. My issue was every behavior I had observed. Everything I remembered. Don't misunderstand, while my father as a man had flaws, as a father, he taught loved and parented within his capacity. My mother honored this in my childhood and continued into my adulthood. What I came to know and understand about him as a man was from my observations. She never demeaned or degraded and to this day still hasn't. Remember I told you before how awesome she was about standing in the folds for me? My mommy is just amazing.

In December of 2008 on my birthday, my cell phone was disconnected. When I came home from work on my birthday, my daughter told me, my sister, Sabrina needed me to call her immediately. I called her back from our home phone.

It was my birthday! I was confident the urgency *was* Sabrina, my baby sister wanting to go over the top to tell me happy birthday as she does every year. She outdid herself in 2008 with birthday wishes! She revealed to me she was pregnant. It was the most fabulous news I heard in a while. My little sister was having a baby. I was excited. About an hour later, my grandma Mildred, my mother's mother called. She said my father wanted me to call him. Well, I always got a call from him on my birthday. Since our argument, we had not spoken in several weeks since he hung up on me. I was sure calling grandma Mildred was his way of reaching out to me. Due to my respect for adults into my adulthood, I would do what it was she asked. So I called. I remember the conversation as I remember everything I recalled earlier. He was my father, the first man to hold my heart and everything he did or said was etched right there.

Coldly I responded after his hello, "Yes. You wanted me to call you?"

"I need to tell you something."

"Ok, what?"

"I just want to apologize for all the pain I have ever caused you. I never meant to hurt you. You know daddy loves you, right?"

"I know… just tell me."

"I have cancer."

"WHAT!"

"I have known since October, and it has spread now."

I remember as if it happened a few minutes into me writing the words. I still get the heaviness in my stomach when I recall the conversation. I forgot it was my birthday at that moment. I forgot all the things I remembered about the drinking, child support, criminal domestic violence or even being embarrassed as a teenager about his drunkenness. I remembered he loved me. I was reminded of all his choices and decisions; he still loved me. I had fed the pit bull of hurt so long I forgot he loved me. My daddy loved me. Daddy died July 14, 2009. My nephew was born in August weighing 7lbs 14 oz.

I held so tightly to his past, I never once saw the man he was in my presence. I strategized my game around the man he was rather than building a relationship with the man he had become. I was comfortable running the familiar interference of not accepting his calls because I was mad. My absence in his life was good enough repayment for his lack of mine. We both had choices, and I made mine based on his. I had the power to cut him out. I didn't build my game plan around the man who took me with him to teach Sunday School at Shrub Branch Baptist Church when I did not know what Sunday school was. As a child teased at school, I forgot about the man who taught me how to punch someone with a barely opened fist hard enough to make their nose bleed. It came in handy one day too. I focused on the past, I had with him, which was what I chose to remember. It was comfortable to play the opponent who was familiar and showed up more times than not.

Remember I said I believed people could change? He did not change; my theory is still correct. He never changed on me; I changed on him. I never applied my thoughts and theories to myself. That is what happens when you aren't self-aware. I take ownership of my mistake now. I was so comfortable feeling hurt I did not realize I was wrong for so long for not forgiving him. I looked at his past and not his decisions. Remember he cried when I told him I was pregnant in Chapter One?

How dare he want his daughter to grow up and have potential beyond what he knew? How dare he want his grandchild to be able to thrive knowing I was still a hopeless teenager? How dare he be frustrated because now telling me he loved me every chance he could have to mean so much more because I would know the same love and understand his. I was playing on the field with his past though.

I didn't even realize he was quarterbacking the game with new players. I was still playing the alcoholic father who never showed up. I didn't even know he was in the game now when it mattered most. I focused on the hurt and pain of my past with so much intensity I never stopped to realize it was taking away from every moment I had right there in front of me. When you speak credit to your past, you place limits on the potential of your present meeting with your future. As you become unapologetic, understand your designed destiny requires the acceptance of your past. Your past did happen, hence the reason it is your past. Concede it happened, but does not define you. While on your authentic journey to being who you are, always remember, regardless of your struggles the critical thing is you are still here. I had to focus on the time I had with him. Now!

I am not a person who liked visiting hospitals, and he knew this. Even in his incapacitation and breathing tubes, he would mouth for me to go home and get some rest. I would come to the hospital during the middle of the day when no one else was there and sit and watch him sleep. Just to hear him breathe. While he had chemotherapy, I would talk with him on Tuesdays on my 30-minute commute to work. He would fill me up in six months with everything he wanted to give me for the last 26 years. Just think if I held on to the pain of my past, what would it have done?

The arsenal of our past, when mishandled and misused can destroy the atmosphere for anything living when you bring up it up. While moving forward in life, it is ok to be unapologetically over some things. It does not justify them; it merely means you permit yourself to move on. Going through something does not always mean you are over it either. Before you cue Elsa and "Let it Go," there are some things we let go of we when we need closure.

My Daddy had to apologize to my sister and I because he had to for where he was in his life. Being the parent, he was, he knew he needed to do it for ours as well. Distinguish what things in your past require closure and what requires you just to wash your hands and walk away. You know the "things." Those things in your past you have become comfortable and complacent sitting with continuously. If you have ever tried to end a conversation about your past saying it-is-what-it-is or "whatever!" Pump the brakes. That's the situation. There are some situations we truly believe we have to let go, put the water back under the bridge and there is no love lost over it. Ask yourself if you dealt with the real issue? Finalization is a part of the process for everything life, a beginning and an ended. Look at where things started to understand how they end. Walking around like you have let it go into this far off mysterious place may make you look good on the outside, but on the inside, that thing is still growing, decaying and waiting to come out. Then eventually, it floats back into the atmosphere at some point, and you are wondering, from where. When it comes back, it sometimes comes back in the same or different form. You take all the stuff you "let go" into your next relationship, to your next job and even in your conversations with the next person who calls your phone. You say hello with an attitude because the last caller just made you mad, but you let it remember?

I think there are some things you should just walk away from, but to be a better person, close the wound and heal, you will have to treat it. You have to address the issue. It may just need reconciliation to you. When my Daddy died, I was already in the midst of dealing with my medical problems. The sicker I felt, the less I went around him. I described earlier on the little man knocking on the inside of my head to get out. On April 14th, 2009 I suffered a Transient Ischemic Attack or Mini Stroke. Between April and July, my visits were few. I made as many phone conversations as I possibly could. I was diagnosed with a brain aneurysm in June of 2009 after I neglected to follow up as instructed in April after my TIA stroke. Here I was a trooper. I was making all my appointments, working a full-time job, just finishing up graduate school and being a wife and mother all at the same time. In my mind, everything was ok, and I was moving on. I was doing what I needed to do. When everyone asked how I was, I would say I was okay. If you didn't need to know I was sick, well, you didn't.

A little over a year after my father passed, I was in my bedroom folding clothes. I could not bring myself to tears when he did pass; I prepared. I was ready. No need to cry or "cut a monkey," – this means acting out if you're from the deep South. *"It is what it is."* I realized at that moment in my bedroom; I was standing in the same spot I was when we had that horrible conversation. The one that caused him to hang up. I was folding clothes from the same small white basket when I told him everything I had been holding in for 26 years.

With no warning at that very moment, in my bedroom all alone, I broke. My husband was in the living room, and my children were in their rooms clueless about what was taking place. I snapped and gasped for air because he was gone. All the things I needed to hear him say over and moreover again, I thought hearing them in the last six months was enough. I thought I was over it. I thought we made up. He was gone. I never got to tell him I was sorry and I did not mean what I said that day. I never got to say to him I was holding all his past against him, but I only remembered what I needed to justify my feelings. I wanted my Daddy; I just kept saying, *"He's gone."* In full transparency, as I type, there is a lump in my throat because I still want him, but he's gone.

Some situations, you were never supposed to be involved with to have residual issues from in the first place. You were, and you do. Accept your past. Know it happened. Grow because it happened. Love because it happened. As hard as it may be, you may have to leave because it happened. Stop because it happened and let go because it is the past. Yes, except you have a mess from your past, issues in your present and some things waiting for you when you get where you are going in the future. Be consistent with the change process.

When playing against our greatest opponents,

God has a touchdown celebration prepared. Waiting in the end zone are bands, cheerleaders, fireworks, music, confetti, and cake. I know there is no cake in football, but I like cake, and this is my book.

Your opponent is between you and the end zone, eyeing you while you are eyeing God. Whatever the enemy is your past, shame, hurt or fear. Whatever your opponent is, he is watching the indecisive shift of your weight and waiting. Watching to see what foot you bring forward and even taunting you in whispers. He is telling you;

"You will never make it."

"Nobody is helping you get there; no one is blocking for you."

"Your sideline is filled with people not paying attention and waiting to get in and replace you."

"You are just a rookie, some kid off the bench; you are not cut out for this."

Sometimes, we believe the opponent. We take a step back. Get comfortable. We focus on the fumbles and interceptions. We second guess the pep talk from the huddle and fundamentals of the playbook. We overlook God already giving us his pep talk based on the strategy he developed for us. God said, "I will block for you. I will open a hole for you. I will carry you to the end zone. I will pull you into the end zone. You do not have to run; you can walk. You do not have to walk; you can crawl. You just have to keep moving. You have to come to me. You have to keep your eyes on me! Do not listen to the crowd in the stands, the people on the sideline calling their plays."

God is telling you, "Stop letting the Goliath of a Devil make you fearful. You covered already. The opponent may tug at you, catch you and even tackle you, but get up and start the play over. Get up and go again. The opposition will not get tired; he will not give up. I promise you; he will never step foot into my end zone to take any of what I promised you away. It is all yours because I SAID SO!"

Down, set, PRAY!

Let's GO!

CHAPTER FOUR
THE ART OF SPEAKING ON PURPOSE

Audacity. The word in itself makes me feel I should write it on the page differently. Remember, I like to perform word autopsies. *Merriam Webster* defines audacity as a confident and daring quality often seen as shocking or rude. Rather than use the word audacity, most people describe the person as being bossy or having an attitude. I have been defined at times as the "Angry Black Woman" or the one with an attitude. I receive the description of having an attitude more often. I have an issue with my facial expressions which seem to get me in a lot of trouble. I have been working on this for years. Had it been my real job I would have been fired a long time ago had it been my real job. People who dare to live unapologetically in their purpose are never usually seen as "go-getters."

They are rarely defined as advocates for themselves or the voice of reason when faced with opposition. I am usually the person in the room who looks at things differently and acts outside the box in unconventional methods or plans of execution. I am not boasting, but most of the time it works. My life requires me to do things differently. Unapologetically, I have to be bold and state the things most people are afraid to acknowledge or even think about in most situations. My purpose requires it. My life needs it.

Nothing hurts more than words unsaid as they lumped in your throat and you push them back down. They usually sit there and turn into bitterness, hurt, rage, depression, and anger. Often, I find when I am deliberate about stating what it is I want it increases the likelihood of me getting much more significant than when I say nothing. I learned the art of speaking intentionally from my great-grandmother Lottie Davis.

We called my great-grandmother, Big Mama. She once was a school teacher, but by the time I was old enough to spend time with her and make memories, she was retired and not moving around as she once did. She was in her early 80s when I was five. She taught many people in the educational setting as well as through her role as a Sunday, school teacher. She loved teaching and had such a calm, sweet spirit.

The older Big Mama got, she began to walk with a cane and was limited in her ability to move around much. She had special places designated for her to sit. You could find her at the far end of the couch, front porch in her white rocking chair, on a stool in the kitchen or the white wooden bench on the carport. She was consistent with certain things. Her consistency growing up provided comfort when we came home from school to her. There were six of us all different ages. There was my sister Sabrina and me and my cousins, Eunice, Larry Jr., Joy and Breeland. The beautiful part of my memories with Big Mama is I don't remember her raising her voice to scream or yell. Every afternoon you could count the six of us in the yard or the house. It never failed that were all six there being loud, dirty, sweaty, crying, laughing and singing all over the place. I don't even remember her yelling for us to come in or stay out of the house. When she spoke, we listened.

The splendor of her voice would lead you to her lap or right there at her feet to hear what she had to say or what she needed. She was deliberate in everything she said to us. She made sure to teach us any and everything she could. Never reading a book or writing anything down, she spoke to us in her soft, sweet voice which we committed to our hearts and still cherish now more than 30 years later. She would give us chores with instruction and once completed she would provide us with more. I remember having many conversations with her while completing tasks as she gave us instructions on the many days we spent with her after school and in the summer.

My sister, Sabrina, cousin Eunice and I would spend the night with Big Mama every chance we could. Mostly it was on Friday and Saturday nights. Big Mama would send us to the store for a kiwi and Baby Ruth candy bar. We would grease her hair with Blue Magic Bergamot hair grease, then roll it with sponge rollers. I still remember the smell of the grease. My lesson in deliberately speaking came when she prayed one Friday night after we were all tucked into bed. We did the regular routine of locking the doors, and we all slept in the room with Big Mama.

While in the bed the house was quiet. There was only a dim night table lamp illuminating Big Mama's face while she sat on the edge of her side of the bed. She began to pray. There was a stillness in the house. We all knew to "just be" until done. Big Mama prayed for every one of her children by name. She then prayed for every one of her grandchildren by name. Big Mama then prayed for every one of her great-grandchildren by name. She just prayed. It was not a long prayer, but only a simple conversation between her and God. We were privileged to be in her presence to hear.

I can only recall feeling the presence of God as I did that night once. I was an adult and the lessons Big Mama taught me were a part of my core values, but I admit, not my everyday practice. One day when I felt everything was closing in on me from stress at work I was re-introduced to God's presence. I had bottled words in for so long, and I felt I was losing my mind at this point. I remembered Big Mama that day. Then, in silence, I left my desk at work and walked outside. I couldn't find the still quiet I did in the room with her that night. I was standing outside, but everything seemed to be again closing in on me and fast. I could scream, curse and yell if I wanted. That was acceptable. I was mad and overwhelmed and excused by yelling and throwing things. I was sure to get a reaction from others, and they would help! I walked.

Further down to the end of the sidewalk, I went to the end of the building. I pushed my back up against the brick wall and began to sink down. Then, I decided at that moment to use my voice and pray. I had to be deliberate in my speaking. I needed to speak to God exactly what I needed from him. I stood and turned my face to the wall. My arms balanced me up, my face full of tears and I screamed out for God to help me. I whispered I needed him…right now. I cannot say I ever prayed to God the way I prayed that day against the wall and it did not matter. I knew I needed to speak to him like Big Mama did that Friday night and asked for what I needed.

See, when Big Mama prayed she was particular with her words. She was thoughtful when she called each name. She made sure to go in the appropriate order and make her request known to God. Her conversation with him was intentional. I have always taken with me the understanding of her knowing precisely the request she was making to God. When she got to the end she said, *"Lord, let thy will be done."* Remembering how she prayed on my journey provided me with an understanding and appreciation to be deliberate with my prayers. Not just my words and petitions to God, but also in the words I speak in my life. Being intentional in speaking sets a standard for what you deem acceptable from others. I have to make decisions about what happens and how I move forward in my life daily. I am deliberate in the things I say, and with every effort, I make clear decisions when choosing what needs to happen to move forward.

My prayers to God were a petition for help. I asked for what I needed. I didn't know what His plans were; I just knew mine wasn't working. To request his will be done I needed to arrive at an unapologetic place. Setting your standards one of the most important things you can do for your life. Articulating what you expect from others and relationships is your request for them to honor you. You're setting the standard of how you honor yourself. Most detrimental on your journey is your inability to speak with purpose. For every time you do not speak, you lose the power to set the standard for your life. It is like handing someone else the keys to your car and letting them take you for a ride. If you do it enough times, you never get your keys back. You just simply own a vehicle you never drive. Setting the standard for expectation for others and what is acceptable for you as well comes from speaking with audacity. I told you earlier about my facial expressions. I am still working on them.

While I am cognizant of my facial expressions, they never really tell you what is indeed happening in my thought process. I was told by a trusted professional mentor my facial expressions bother other people. I never really smile. So my phone conversations work better. Here is the thing; it goes back to my ability to speak deliberately. While my face may look as though I am upset, my words may tell you otherwise. It is why I deliberately speak sets my standard. What resonated from the conversation I had with this particular individual was the statement that I "had to play the game." Well, what in the world does that mean? Play the game? If there is one thing I cannot do, it is playing the game. I began to realize why it did not make sense when provided to me at the time in my life. I was on a journey to be unapologetic. I set a standard to be authentic and real with others, regardless of the cost. Therefore "playing the game" was not something I could at all do or tolerate.

Unapologetically speaking existence into what I wanted to see and outcomes I desired, would not line up with me playing the game, with anyone. I learned the power of my words very quickly. As a writer, I understood how cathartic writing was for me. I felt a release of emotion and stress when I wrote. While I found the words to write, I never really noticed my voice until I decided to be true to myself. After my transient ischemic attack or mini-stroke in 2009, I realized writing was not working. I was working as a full time professional in child protective services, married with two daughters and a son who just turned one. In February my father who was diagnosed and receiving treatment for cancer was hospitalized from a fall. I was keeping everyone ok. I wanted to make sure I spent and communicated with my Daddy as much as I could.

I spent much of my time the few weeks before my stroke attempting to keep it together. I was writing everything I felt and needed to release, but I still had no voice. On the outside, I looked like I had it together, but on the inside, I was like a carbonated drink being shaken vigorously back and forth. After my mini-stroke on April 14th, 2009, the doctor said for me to see my family doctor. What did the emergency room people know? I would just follow up with my family doctor when it was time for my next physical in June. Naomi did not have time for that.

Hours after my annual physical exam in June, my family doctor made an immediate appointment for me the following day with the Neurologist upon review of my April x-ray. Then for more scans and x-rays, I would be sent. Still battling and moving forward, my husband and I took a family vacation with the children to Myrtle Beach. It was the first family vacation we had taken, and we enjoyed ourselves. I loved lying on the beach under the umbrella; the sun is beaming in just a little, while the wind blew. Something was relaxing about the smell of salt water in the air as I listened to my daughters laugh and watched my son play in the sand. We played in the water and the sand with enjoyment.

I remember realizing how relaxed and calm I felt. I remember thinking "I needed this vacation." We returned home after a few days and prepared to go to Carowinds the next morning. While I unpacked, I sat on my husband's side of the bed and checked the answering machine. I played several messages that were irrelevant and then I heard one from the neurologist office. *"Mrs. Washington, we need you to call us back. It is urgent."* I called back, and she asked, *"Are you at home alone?"* I told her I was not as I walked into the room with my husband. I told her my husband was with me, and he looked up at me from the computer wondering to who I was speaking. I placed the call on speaker phone at the time she was saying, *"The scans of your brain revealed an aneurysm."* I don't recall much of the conversation after those words. My husband continued the conversation with her while I sat and looked straight forward into his face.

No high blood pressure, a few headaches here and there, but nothing rest did not resolve. There were no symptoms at all. No signs. I was dealing with a little stress, but nothing out of the ordinary. I had been dealing with the same stressful co-workers and the job environment for over three years. I kept telling myself I was ok, but what did I bottle? Before the stroke, I dealt with things on the inside because I did not know how to deal with them on the outside. It was horrible because the things I needed to say the most, I didn't. I was attempting to salvage the emotions and feelings of others by maintaining my hurt.

Remember the carbonated drink. I was shaking it up for almost three years and refused to open the lid. On the outside, I was careful in what I did or did not say, but I was dismissing and shaking up the drink with my caution. I had to be cautious of everyone's feelings. Who was I to play the victim? Don't forget I was also playing a football game with my past and it was winning. I was still holding on to what I felt I deserved. I was silently shaking myself up with stress to the point a brain aneurysm in the front right hemisphere of my brain had the potential to explode. The carbonated drink formed in a blood vessel in my brain.

I was allowing stress to fill up an aneurysm and then letting it settle right back down. It explained later to me by the radiologist I only had the option of surgery. I could potentially live with an aneurysm, but if it burst and I didn't die, I would be blind in the right eye. So I was faced with the harsh reality of my choices. I could write and have relief, but with no voice, I could potentially lose my life or my vision. Looking back, God was telling me because I did not speak, I was already dead.

I had already lost my vision every time I shook myself up with stress. I took an inventory over my life and realized some of the reasons I was holding my words was because I valued others more than I appreciated myself. I would much rather live in the silent lie of being ok than have them live in the truth of the pain they caused me. Hurt by people's words and actions for so long, I was shutting down and holding things in became how I communicated with others. All of the stress began to suffocate me one day. My only option was to get my voice. God took me to the wall. That day I faced a wall outside the office where co-workers were becoming more vindictive and prayed deliberately to God because my Daddy was dying, my surgery delayed, my co-workers labeled me "Angry Black Woman," I was virtually dead.

After my surgery to coil an aneurysm in my brain, I spent the night alone in the ICU. I was carrying too much emotional weight and baggage because of the words I did not release. Between my consultation on July 8th and my procedure on August 31th my aneurysm had doubled in size from stress. I was choosing to write and caution my words which was apparently not working well for me. It was in the ICU on August 31, 2009; I had my conversation with God. I talked to him just as Big Mama did. I was deliberate in my words. I was intentional in every petition for my family, and in the end, I asked, "Let thy will be done." I had to be deliberate. My life and sanity depended on me being deliberate in my words at that moment.

Beginning that day, I unapologetically made a conscious effort to be deliberate in not only what I said, but what I allowed others to tell me as well. I had to be deliberate in what I prayed and asked of God. There was a time when I let the words of others build or tear me down because I did not know the power of my words over my life. It was like I would blow up a balloon and people close enough in my life would come along and deflate it.

A brain aneurysm was never designed to kill me at 27. It did not develop to take my vision either. God wanted me to use my voice. I needed to have the audacity to live my life differently. I needed to boldly acknowledge the last 26 years of my life were not the last 26 years of my life. I had so much to live for, and it was time to live unapologetically authentic in all I was designed to be.

Everything which happens does not have to keep repeating. The cultural and societal norm of women and girls not being bold and speaking up unfortunately still exist. Then for a woman of color, it brings about a whole different stereotype and stigma. I lost my voice a long time ago in an attempt to fit in. I see it so often in others. There are so many things people endure in life from their family cycles and out of ignorance which does not have to keep happening. As a young girl, I remember sitting in church wondering how old I had to be before I was supposed to wear hats to church. Not that I wanted to wear a hat to church, it just seemed to be what was happening. The cycle continues. What in your life remains a cycle? Finding my voice in the ICU afforded me a strength I never thought I ever possessed. I controlled my life. I realized if I was deliberate and asked for what I wanted or needed from others, I just might get it. If I stepped up to advocate for myself, I might just move forward to be in the position I want for my life.

While authentic living requires you to determine and set the standard for what is acceptable in your life from others and to others, it does begin the shift. Being deliberate in your speaking engages active accountability to the standard you set. I received an e-mail from another professional during the process of writing this book which insulted me. After having two other people read the e-mail without letting them know my thoughts, they acknowledged the e-mail was condescending and patronizing. I revisited my previous e-mail and felt I set the tone for the conversation by outlining my request for additional information. I articulated the plan developed for the particular project I was working on at the time. Now I am at a crossroad.

Do I respond by "giving her the business" as the kids say? I decided not to respond. While I have found my voice and know the importance of having it, I know when I should and should not use it as well. By not acknowledging the e-mail, tone, and statements made towards me, I set the standard through my silence that it was unacceptable. I owe it to my authentic self to remain silent at a time when I want to establish who I am to this particular person by replying. Simply stated, I have the right to remain silent because anything I say can and will be used against me as I strive towards my purpose and the perception I carry with me. Unapologetically live in the knowledge that just because everyone else did it and did it for so long, does not make it right for you. Proverbs 18:2, *"A fool takes no pleasure in understanding, but only in expressing his opinion."* There is no need to engage in a war of words to solidify your position on anything. While it may work in certain situations to go back and forth, you gain nothing but position. We have established that life is not about your position but instead your purpose

Each of our lives is different by design. While

will working and creating your standard of what works best for you, you have to move beyond what you have already learned. I may never wear a hat to church, and it does not make me any less of a believer than the woman in front of me with one. While I respect the tradition, it is not for me.

Living in my purpose charges me to speak differently. When a child is born, they begin to make noises which turn into words. Words then become sentences and sentences become conversations. When you walk in your purpose, it looks the same way. You begin to speak of your dreams which develop into your speaking of goals. Expressed goals turn into deliberate actions and actions open the opportunity to celebrate the achievement. All the while, learning to speak unapologetically deliberately.

You can never get back the words you release. The most powerful thing we have is our word. I can speak success or defeat of myself. I can talk my way out of a ticket or talk my way into an arrest. I can speak my way into a million-dollar job or speak my way out of one. I can speak positive thoughts to the people around me or with every negative thing I say, break them down to deplete their worth.

Every day I am learning and making an effort to choose my words wisely. I have learned the importance of being true to myself with an affirmation to "Say what you mean." I am learning to be clear and deliberate in my conversations with others and my relationships. The best way to do this is first with me. One of the hardest people to be true with is you. I had to come to terms in my self-reflection about what I wanted and needed to communicate it with others. I had to "say what you mean" to myself. If I cannot be real with anyone, I know I can be real with Naomi. I do have to check myself sometimes. I have to remind myself to "get out of your feelings; this is not about you." "This is not your issue to fix." "Don't go there right now, fall back."

Deciding to be deliberate in my words with others and even with myself required me to be consistent in my actions as well. Big Mama made her petitions to God, but I could see it in her care and concern for each of the persons for whom she prayed. It was not a prayer; she decided she would do and leave it at his feet, she paid attention. She may have a few favorite places to sit, the rocker on the porch, the far end of the couch and stool in the kitchen, but from where she was she had access to all and all had access to her. If I was encouraging others with my words, I must also be supportive in my actions. I have to be deliberate in what I am going to communicate as acceptance for my life and make consistent decisions that mirror my communication. Your actions speak louder than anything you could ever communicate with someone.

You must speak to yourself with confidence. Always speak with certainty. You will not know how to operate your life until you say what it is you want and desire for yourself. You have to say what you mean by the declaration.

"I WANT to be loved."

"I WANT better for my family."

"I WANT to be successful."

Tasked with being as authentic with yourself as you would anyone else is already given to you.

"I DO NOT WANT to fail."

"I DO NOT WANT to live unfulfilled."

It is most beneficial to you and the people in your life for you to do this. It is when we say what we "mean," can we get what we "want." As I write this book, I say what I mean to myself each time I sit at this computer. I owe it to myself and you to consistently and deliberately speak. I want you to read this. I want you to like it, but not as much as I want you to grow from it. I charge you to say what you mean to yourself.

Stop saying everything is fine when you know it is not. Stop telling yourself you are ok when you are not. Stop saying you are not capable of doing something when you have not tried. Do not play with your words, speaking uncertainty into situations or deliberate deceit into some of the purest intentions of others and opportunities presented to you. SAY WHAT YOU MEAN.

CHAPTER FIVE
STAND UP TO STAND OUT

Have you ever wondered "Why am I here?" Sometimes the questioning is literal and at other times more introspective. You may have a successful job and love being a spouse, and a parent with significant relationships and life looks fantastic on paper, but yet still you want to know why you are here. You may wonder at times what the real reason is for your life. We spend all our time caring for others, all the while neglecting ourselves. In the titles and responsibilities, we still sometimes find ourselves wondering if we even scratched the surface of our own lives.

As a child, I often wondered times if there was anything special about me as a person. I often wondered what exactly I would be to the world. I looked like my father, who no one ever said anything good about, at least not to me. I looked different from my classmates who picked on me because I was lighter skinned, wore thick glasses, had thick hair and needed braces. I even had a Jheri Curl once. I was quiet and did not speak much in school and always had a grimace on my face. I was not the most popular girl and undoubtedly was not the smartest. I remember asking God on several occasions, "Why am I here?" I remember moments I would scream to God, "WHY AM I HERE?" Indeed, if anyone knew, He knew! I just needed Him to tell me. I needed to know right there at that moment. Some of those moments when I asked were moments I did need to know. I needed him to tell me the reason was more than the moment. The reason was more than what others were telling me, and in his silence, I was beginning to believe them. I needed to know.

As I look back on those moments now, I realize he never intended to answer me. I have those moments with my children as well. They ask me questions, and I do not answer only because I know it is not the time. When my son was five, he asked, *"Where do babies come from?"* That is a question most parent's dread hearing. There is no way to answer a five-year-old, truthfully and just end the conversation. My husband always defers those questions to me and then patiently smiles and watches as I struggle to change the conversation. "Oh, look *Insert some random boy thing here that pulls his attention away. The older he gets the mother the tactic doesn't work.

So here I am as the child asking God, *"Why am I here"* and like a parent with the "baby" question, he is changing the subject. I am not ready for the answer. If he answers, I will have more questions. If he answers, I will not understand how the process takes place. I will tell him why it will hurt, not work, be an ugly process and how impossible it is. So, in time, he can only answer me in small ways. He can just respond to me by saying when I am ready, he will tell me. When I need the answers, I will receive them.

How often have you sought your purpose? Your purpose is not just something you are good at doing. I have mastered the art of making spreadsheets. That is not my purpose. Although I make spreadsheets for work, it's not my job. It is the means by which I fulfill my obligation. Sometimes we confuse what we are good at with what we are called to do. Just because you enjoy doing something, does not make it your purpose. I am almost sure the worst cook in the world is in a kitchen somewhere right now, cooking their little heart out, and it's just not their purpose. They can love it all they please want, but love doesn't mean cooking is their purpose. If the cook is you, I am sorry, walk in your truth!

Our purpose is what we are consistently called back to doing. I can be at my worst moments or my best moments, and I write. I can be driving down the interstate and be drawn to write. Safely on the side of the road, I might add. It is the thing you put down a long time ago because you did not do it as well as others, but it keeps calling you back. For all those times I asked God why am I here and he never answered, he was preparing me for moments such as this. While there was a significant need to know what my purpose was, I first needed to accept I had a purpose at all. My purpose was in clear contrast to the messages around me. My reason for asking was not because I needed to know, but because I could not see it or at least not in the moments when I asked him the questions.

We see things in our lives, keeping us busy and discouraged. Every day I see images reminding me of everything I am not. I see images telling me that greatness does not look like me. God could not answer me. What I was seeing was not going to align with whatever answer, he provided to me at the moment. Once I began to accept I was more than what I saw, I was able to understand a little better. I intentionally made an effort to surround myself with things that lined up with what the vision was for my life. That is right; I developed a vision. I realized I needed to embrace and love myself moments I did not know my purpose. My purpose was the only way I was going to move forward to be a better person. I began to see things differently. What is your vision for your life?

Your vision should propel you to focus on intentional alignment. You are the architect of your vision. Architects draw blueprints and ultimately become responsible for executing the collaboration with those who will build the structure. Architects must research to find the right locations and materials. They work for the right contractors and companies to perform the labor and day to day task of the build. The consider individuals who will consistently oversee the daily changes and progress made or not made. They must often make changes and adjustments due to variables out of their control. All the while maintaining the vision of what will be the end project. Are you prepared and accepting of the requirements to be who you are on purpose?

When I contemplated doing a blog, I asked my close friend, Christalyn who would read it. Her reply was simple from the cubicle behind me, *"The world."* My view at the time was of the cubicle in front of me. While all I could see was the current situation of my life, I never second-guessed my ability to reach anyone outside of the cubicle. My vision was to inspire others on their journey. My purpose was to motivate and encourage others to a new place within themselves. Can you imagine if Christalyn did not like me and told me I was right and just to keep writing in my journal? What if I did not believe her at all and just kept doing what I thought I was equipped to do? It took courage to stand up and say I am going to start a blog. It took courage to say I am going to write about my real-life experiences. I had to stand out and say I was going to be the one to write a blog about being angry, hurt and happy. I had to be authentic. If I was going to live my purpose, I had to stand out.

I knew writing was my gift. I knew a long time ago; it was what God blessed me to do. I was not confident in the gift. I always thought the gift was for me and never realized the gift was really for others. I was not aware at the time in my life what purpose meant. I was still stumbling around on a day to day basis in what I could see and never really took the time to have a vision. If God created me for anything other than writing, it simply was out of the question. If you remember I told you I had a lot of issues in my past that proved I was not qualified to be the person who stood out from the crowd. I was never supposed to be the one who was successful. I was a teen mother, and I was a single mother. I was not the most popular or the smartest academically. I believed those things. Those same things still creep up in my mind now as I write. I think the only person who is going to read this book is my Mommy and only because she is my Mommy.

One of the many things I learned very quickly with God was to be confident in his abilities. Everything I am not equipped to do is because he has not prepared me yet "May God give you every good thing you need so you can do what He wants. May He do in us what pleases Him through Jesus Christ. May Christ have all the shining-greatness forever! Let it be so. (Hebrews 13:21New Life Version NLV)" Did you know when you are what God has fashioned you to be you know the only one who has a problem with it is the enemy? The enemy does not like you because he does not even like himself. My love for reading introduced me to authors and writers as a child still unknown to some adults my age. If I had never known who Nikki Giovanni was, I might have never decided on writing poems at all. None of what God has laid out in His blueprint was by accident. I hope you believe this to be true. Nothing he has designed and set out before you on your journey is to fail but designed to build your faith. Standing out and standing up requires you to be confident. What is it you are putting off doing because of fear? What is it you have already deemed yourself to be inadequate or undeserving of accomplishing? That is the very thing God will use to put you before others in victory for His glory. What you are worried others will use to disqualify you is the very thing he created to set you apart. I have seen him prepare a table in front of my enemies. He even made some of them get up from the table.

    I was participating in a small group at church. My mentor was leading the group, and I revealed to them, I write, but others are not allowed to read it. It was almost like me saying, I cook well, but no one can eat it. I did not deny my gift was my ability to write. However, I continued to diminish the value of what I was writing. It was my answers to the questions I asked you earlier, which resulted in me taking a back seat in my purpose. I was inadequate and unqualified to have others become inspired by anything I wrote. Those same reasons were what God used to set me apart. Yesterday happened the way it did so today could happen the way it should. Here is the secret; for your purpose, you are already qualified. We just have to stand up and stand out to believe it ourselves. When you predicate your actions, decisions, and control over to anyone other than God you turn your blessings into burdens. Had I not gone through those moments of answering those very questions I asked earlier, you may not be reading this book. I had to clear the atmosphere intentionally!

Standing up requires us to clear the atmosphere of everything holding us back. You have no plan B! There is no other option other than to stand up and stand out boldly, authentically and unapologetically in your purpose. Can you imagine what you could be doing right at this very moment if you cleared your thought pattern and changed your behaviors? Boldly you would be standing in your purpose when others needed to lean on you.

You are required to clear the atmosphere intentionally. Let's say we are taking a flight. For you to take this flight, you need to be ready to launch, but how many of us worry about the crash? Not even off the ground yet and we anticipate our demise. If we go a little deeper, we probably have passengers on our flights who are not qualified to be on the plane. They got on our flights with their flight plans and fears. Some people are under the influence. However, we allow them to take a window seat and hold the intercom on our journey. Here we are afraid to crash not even leaving the runway. Who do you have to escort off your plane's flight manifesto? I have been there, afraid to crash when I had not launched yet. I had too much weight on my plane. I was taking along everyone else's insecurities and beliefs about my launch. For you to start your life, you need to focus on one thing and one thing only at this point. You!

Making sure you have a transparent atmosphere for your launch is a priority. I guess you are wondering why the atmosphere is so vital regarding our flight. Unfortunately, in flying there could potentially be issued when you are in midflight. So if we took the time to assess the atmosphere beforehand, it would alleviate additional issues. That just means, changing your patterns. I already know when I get uncomfortable with things I want to quit and give up. So I have intentionally decided in my life when things get uncomfortable, I have to send a distress call to those close to me. Those people who will call me out on this self-sabotaging behavior and encourage me to keep going. Even the encourager needs to be sometimes encouraged. Be prepared to deal with your issues. That's right, get out of your way.

Every pilot radios back to the traffic controller for guidance. Are you using yours? There are people on your journey at different stages. Some have had flights that were smooth, and others just came out of the storm towards which you are heading. There are some people ready to launch, while others are already in flight. While you are entirely responsible for your course, you are still able to take direction and guidance from those who are also traveling on their own as well. You also have an obligation to those who are yet waiting in the wings to launch. You provide them with the same guidance and support offered to you. Some people are already at the point of landing, but keep making circles. There are some who are nose down, wheels up, ready to land. There are people prepared to launch into new careers, stagnant in current relationships or anticipating a life-changing experience with no positive outlook. What they need is for you to stand out! How you launch will affect your travel and how you travel will change how you land. You have to decide if you are willing to launch. What is stopping you? You have evaluated the passengers, you know your destination, and you see the flight plan. What is stopping you now?

Be OK in your season with your growth. Understand everything God gives you has a season and will produce fruit at the appointed time. It's your time to be the person you were destined to be. Be conscious of the distractions. No more wavering back and forth with what others expect of you. It is time to stop fighting the deep down desires. While it may seem as though you are going against everything you see, you must speak unapologetically about the person you are destined to be in the future. Unapologetically accept you are wonderfully made and created with a specific and unique gift only you possess. Right now, at this moment, there should be a sense of urgency to stand up and stand out. You have felt it before, and you knew it because of your purpose. You do certain things differently. You are set apart in a rather peculiar way and draw people to you because of your purpose. 1 Peter 2:9-10 The Message (MSG) *"But you are the ones chosen by God, chosen for the high calling of priestly work, chosen to be a holy people, God's instruments to do his work and speak out for him, to tell others of the night-and-day difference he made for you—from nothing to something, from rejected to accepted."*

It is time for you to unapologetically prepare and accept every requirement to be who you are on purpose. Do not spend so much time focusing on the struggle until you lose faith in what you are striving. When you focus on your future, you don't have time to worry about the past.

Can you imagine all the people tied to your purpose? My grandmother and great aunt always ask for the same thing for Christmas, dish detergent, washing powder, soap, toilet paper and paper towels. Every year this is what they list in their response when asked what they would like for Christmas. It has gotten to the point where I don't ask. They are very appreciative of the gifts they are given if not from the list, but when asked this is what they want. As a child, they would purchase us underwear. We would be so embarrassed and save the gift for last because we all knew they gave underwear. The children would un-wrap gifts and hold them up for everyone to see and then someone would un-wrap the underwear. When I look back, underwear was the best gift for us growing children. If you asked me what toys I received, I probably couldn't tell, you but I still remember getting underwear. I have a Christmas photo holding up pajamas with the feet in them. I was excited! Just looking at the photo, I feel warm and cozy inside. You know you do too just thinking about them. My elders, stood in their roles to provide for me what I needed even when I didn't know it. I am responsible for this very same thing in my purpose.

All the people who need you to be in a position so they can finish their course of life are waiting. Had my writing coach decided to be a fitness trainer, you may not be reading this book. If my husband decided to join the military, I probably wouldn't be his wife. If my mother decided to go back to live in Philadelphia early on in her life, I might not be here now. If you want to be more specific, just think, had I not shown up in my purpose anything you have gained from these pages, would not have happened. Someone depends on me to write this chapter and this very sentence.

Through all the delays and procrastination, I still have to come back to the place designed and ordained for me. I have a mission. I must stand in my place. Beyoncé calls it "Formation." If I never walk unapologetically into my purpose, someone will never receive what it is in me, for them. God has ordained and orchestrated everything, and the most important part is for you to be in position. It's like a chain reaction. God needs you to be in line with the purpose he has for your life. There is someone else who is depending on you to live out your vision.

Every moment you show up in your purpose aligns with someone needing to show up on their own. Until you start the process of lifting others up, your elevation will not amount to anything. I boldly, unapologetically share my testimony because what I have gone through was sometimes for my good, and even when it was not it has always been for God's glory. There is a point in your life when you have to realize where you are and who you are is not on your merit. God has arranged every opportunity and every person who either entered or exited your life for your purpose. When you find yourself in moments of transition, remember it is all a part of his plan. Will you stand up and stand out for your purpose, TODAY? If you choose to say no, are you prepared to deal with that as well?

CHAPTER SIX
MAKE THE CHOICE

In January 2016, I became the CEO of NewPlaceWithin, LLC. I stepped out on faith and became a business owner. It has been one of the most interesting and foreign things I have ever had to do. I have a degree in social work and human services. Therefore, business is not my expertise. I am required to fill out paperwork, understand numbers, learn terms and develop contracts. I decided in 2016 to choose to be a business owner finally. I made a choice.

In 2012 when I thought about the idea of becoming an actual business owner, I was consistently asked about my mission statement. I had to venture outside of my writer hat to develop an understanding of business. Once I became familiar with the requirements, it became evident the answer to the question. I had to develop into words the value and belief of my business. Now being compiled into a mission statement have always been there. The statement governs an understanding of everyone working with my business our belief and values. In the beginning stages of developing my mission statement, I wondered why people did not have a mission statement for their lives. Why had I never treated my own life as a business? Why had I not focused on making sure my core values and beliefs were stated and represented in every relationship developed, life-changing decision and when situational transitions arose? When businesses are developing partnerships and transactions, they hold true to the mission and goal of their entities.

How much easier would our lives be if we developed a mission statement? A mission statement would require us to be who we are and purposed to be in life. How many of your decisions and relationships would be easier with a clearer purpose if your mission statement decided them? Ultimately, the business is you. You are working for you. You are working to ensure everyone who encounters your life has a place at the table for your negotiations. How easy would it be to unapologetically end transactions and dissolve relationships based on the understanding your missions are not aligned? "It just is not working out." "This is not a good fit for either of us." "At this time, we will need to part ways." I know, easier said than done.

First, you must start with your mission statement. What is the belief you have in your life? You must unapologetically be willing to live out that belief. No matter how ugly it looks or how hard things may seem, your mission is a foundation for moving forward. Some of the most successful businesses are successful because they hold fast to their mission. Built on faith and customer services,

Chic-Fil-A never opens on Sunday, and you will receive hands down the best customer service in the world. I accept the challenge if you know of a better establishment with customer service. Just e-mail me!

You will never pull up to your favorite fast food restaurant and to purchase furniture. Your favorite news station will never merge into an agreement to sponsor an event not beneficial to the community it serves. Do not compromise your brand, you. I will never agree with anyone who will cause me to lose my mind. My mission is to encourage and support others. If I lose my mind, what good am I to anyone else? My mission is to live unapologetically and authentically in who God has called me to be. I will never use my gift as a means of persuasion to encourage anyone to live their own lives outside of their maximum capacity for greatness. Period. What is your mission statement? The challenge of writing a mission statement is you must give it some thought.

Your mission statement should define your goals and objectives. It should spell out what you want for yourself, your life and what others who experience your presence should receive a return as well. What about you, will enrich and contribute to the lives of others? For some people, it is as simple as being able to smile and brighten the room. For some, it is the gift of singing whenever asked by others who simply need them to sing. My mother in law will bake a red-velvet cake for anyone who asks. If God did not create Mary Washington to do anything else, she has mastered Red Velvet Cake! Your mission statement should demonstrate everything you want to create, achieve and maintain your life. It is the statement by which you will manage and develop your life from this moment forward.

One very important part of your mission statement needing consideration is your image. In 2012, I knew the title of this book before I put the first word on the page. Interestingly enough, I did not have a completed mission statement, but I knew I was Unapologetically Here. I knew someone needed the blueprint for the journey I have and currently continue to date. I prepared for you when you didn't even know it.

In every moment and with every decision I was unapologetically in the position and place I needed to be to live out my destiny. Every image and decision from then on was resting on my being unapologetically in alignment with what God promised me. Every decision professionally, personally and even spiritually was for me to be who I am today in my life. Yes, every mistake and failure I have made since making the decision as well. A mission statement guides us to move forward. The image others have about you should be synonymous with your mission statement. Before you ever speak a word, your image should say what you represent. What images do you portray to others? Is your image one of encouragement, support, and love? Our mission can be one thing, yet the visual representation, we send to others speaks something drastically different.

Mission statements define the roles and development; we establish for ourselves. While my mission is to help others, I often strive to develop my skills and abilities. I have not always been the woman to write the words you read. Some things never articulated about my life are written in this book. I had to grow and become the person in a place to articulate those pieces of information. A part of my journey to authenticity established me being honest about those moments as well. While I know they are difficult for some people to read, they are the perception and truth which has developed me into who I am today. Some things, in all honesty, were just as hard to write out as they were to say to anyone. Are you ready to decide to develop and grow past where you are at this moment right now? Are you ready to acknowledge and position yourself to have joy?

Live your mission statement. Unapologetically live your purpose. There is nothing more important to your life than you. Analyze every relationship and decision by your mission statement. Align yourself with the mission. If you cannot develop a mission statement right now, that is fine. Speak and live one into existence. You are your brand. Do not keep the world waiting for the gifts God has planted in you for his glory. Develop and write a mission statement for every day. What you speak of your life you believe. Be deliberate in speaking your mission statement. Be deliberate in what you speak about yourself. Be deliberate in what you allow others to speak into and over your life. Knowing your mission and understanding your gift is important.

Position yourself for joy when you live unapologetically. There is peace the decision to have joy brings to your life you will need. See, having joy about where your future delays obstacles and detours will not deter your outlook. If I could go back and give my 15-year-old self-advice, I would tell her to find joy. I had my daughter at 16. Now here is the issue. I had more negative predictions placed on me from being a teen mom by older women than from my peers. Today, some of those same older women see me and just radiate with happiness and excitement.

They want to hug and kiss me and see how I am doing all the time. I hate hugs and kisses by the way, but some things had to happen before I could even accept their present-day accolades. See, most of these women spoke of my downfall when I was 16 and pregnant. They predicted my failures to their daughters who were my peers. They ridiculed my mother because of my actions and articulated my future demise before I even graduated high school. In all I became determined. I was determined to inspire myself.

So there I was in a moment of anger, hurt and shame trying to push through not only the transition of being a teen mom but also being a teen making decisions about what I wanted to be when I grew up. I had to decide on colleges and diapers, study for the SAT and teach my daughter to count, color and her alphabet. All the odds were against us. While I wanted to quit, I knew I had to honor my daughter because what she was to become was determined by who I became at this moment. I decided to honor my mother and my great aunt who pushed me to strive for more than spoken words in difficult times over my life. In this crucial time, I realized there will always be people attached to my life who see where I am and not where I am going. There will be people with promises and aspirations for my potential, good or bad.

Later in life, I learned the moment you feel you have to prove your worth to someone is the moment to absolutely walk away from the attachment. I had to disassociate, become blind and mute to the words of much wise and wisdom filled women in my life, community and most of all church.

Everyone will not see your destiny. Everyone will not understand why you move forward when things look impossible. They will never be able to comprehend you are walking out a destiny that looks dusty. They will not be able to explain how your circumstances said no but you heard from somewhere beyond what they were saying. YES! People who see you winning do not understand how because they do not have access to the game plan etched in your heart.

How many times have we heard people on television when describing their near to death experience say they're "lives flashed" before them? I had the feeling when I held each of my children. I held my babies and envisioned their futures full of possibilities and potential. Unfortunately, as most parents do, I blanketed everything I envisioned over them to tell them what they were going to be when they grew up. Just as I have done this to my children, so many people have done this to you and me.

We feel we have to live up to last names and expectations from others. Oh, the dreaded high school superlatives. I was voted most likely to sleep in class and now I cannot catch a nap if it fell on top of me. You probably lived the same way. People around you were almost taking bets on what would happen to you in life because of who your parents were, how much they made and where they went to school. They were anticipating what would be your ultimate success story because of factors you were merely born into and had no control over. Positive or negative, you had predicted outcomes. Then there are the predictions based on your actions and behaviors.

Others will not always understand your mission statement, see your purpose or even acknowledge your gift. What they cannot take from you is your joy. When people around you laugh at your mission, they are not capable of helping you to reach it. My vision to write a book ties to my mission of being great in my capacity. People will limit you to a box. Usually the same box they could never get themselves out of, so they assume you will make great company. Do not share your mission with people not capable fulfilling it.

It's time to make a choice right where you are and at this very moment. It's time for you to decide to live out every word of your mission statement. The time is now for you to run out on every circumstance you felt hostage to for years. Your dreams should always have a vacancy, your motivation always employed and your potential limitless boundaries. Unapologetically decide joy is more important for the person in the mirror to be their proudest every day moving forward. Designed for you to be better with every day is your destiny.

CHAPTER SEVEN
BUILD YOUR SUPPORT NETWORK

If you read the acknowledgments in this book, you see I have several people who helped me reach the place where this book came true. While these individuals have been with me on my journey for several years, there have been others who were only in place for specific reasons and seasons. It was the support and acceptance of everyone on my journey, if only for a day or two, which positioned me to be here today. While each acknowledgment was for this book, some of the same individuals listed, and some who aren't, have been a part of my support network on this journey to be the person I am today.

A huge part of becoming authentic requires a network to include people who genuinely care enough to tell you when you are not true to yourself. I have a select group of confidants for the professional, personal and spiritual areas of my life. I have advisors who nurture, advocate and hold me accountable for being the woman I am. I have learned the people are providing me with the support needed to have three distinct characteristics. They needed to have a genuine interest in my success, knowledge for my journey and confidence in me to provide the support I needed. There are times when I have to trust these individuals more than I trust myself. For example, after having an in-depth conversation with someone in my circle during a difficult time, she said to me, "there is a lesson in what you are going through." She knew I was hurting and needed to feel better. She wanted me to experience the hurt. I needed to experience the hurt. I needed to "sit in my decisions" is how she described it. She promised me as a friend she would be there for me. As someone personally concerned for my growth as a woman, she was not going to intrude on the lesson. She was not going to let me stay down, but I needed to suffer the fall. During this difficult time in my life, my confidence in her never wavered. She never divulged my struggle but held me accountable by telling me when and if I was wrong. She encouraged me to question and never let me abandon the process. I came through it with her support as she promised. She was a listening ear and sounding board, so I did not make decisions without thinking them through.

Make a list of the people in your life that you consider your support. Next, imagine you are writing an acceptance speech for being who you are today. Now, thank everyone who has helped you accomplish this achievement. For both, the positive and the negative, write a "Thank you" to every one of them, specifically for the role they played in your life. Now, without reviewing the first list you have written, imagine the person you hope to become. In the same manner, write an acceptance speech for achieving the goal you desire to accomplish in your life. It can be 50 years, five years or 5 days from now. Again, write a "Thank you," but this time with the people on the second list you believe will need to be involved in your transformation. Are your two lists the same? Do you need to meet some people to help you become who you desire to be in your life? Who has God aligned you with that you may have left off your second list because their value has not reached its fullest potential yet? If you think this part is hard, here is the hard part, let go of anyone who is not on the second list! You read that right. Anyone who cannot help you become the person you desire to don't need to be involved in your life. Harder said than done, right? I know, but what are they pulling from your life's potential. If you have to wonder where you stand with someone, perhaps it is time to stop standing and start walking. Don't let people pull from your supply when they are not willing to restock what they took. Remember when you took that flight a few chapters ago. I am talking about those same people on your airplane. They are high jacking space needed for those people on the second list. Take into account during the day how many people emotionally take from you. Access to your life has been granted to everything and everyone because of the connection to you. They have access to your potential, greatness and even your sanity. Eliminate the excess which has access to your success.

There must be people around you who will

hold you accountable on your journey. When we seek validation from others, we lose our qualifications. Those who hold us accountable must have a right to do so. I only trust certain people in my life to give me their honest opinion. While everyone will have an opinion, only certain people are trusted to have my best interest at heart in any given situation, I can have a conversation with three of my friends and all three, without having a conversation with one another, will tell me the same thing, right or wrong. It never fails. They all tell me the same thing. I trust them to do this when I need it. I trust them to say the things I do not want to hear. Placing trust in them requires me to be a big girl about things. We have a disingenuous habit of calling people haters. It does not hate if that is your stuff, honey. That's your stuff, and you don't want to own it. I do the same for others because I know the value it has added to mine

    Sometimes you have to tell people what they need to hear, not what they want to hear. The truth doesn't scar an open mind. What you hesitate to say to someone says a lot about the relationship. Faith in others is the expectation of their character while our trust is based solely on what they have delivered. Either your support network will drain you or sustain you. Look for completion and not depletion of the people in your circle. Make sure everyone around you has a positive force. Everyone has their force of energy.

While this is the last chapter, it is the most important. Here is where the work begins. Unapologetically embrace your God-given design despite your past. Recover every fumble of your potential and possibility as you defeat your past to your purpose. I pray for you an audacity to speak with boldness everything you need and want for your life with the hope you get it. Here is where you intentionally show up on your mission with the support of a network to fulfill your God designed destiny. Here is where you live, your purpose on purpose. I am unapologetically here. There is no reason you shouldn't be either.

AFTERWORD

"Say what you mean and mean what you say." It's one of those catch phrases that just seem to get to the point. It gets to the heart of the matter. It's what I like to call an AMEN statement.

Naomi Washington is an AMEN kind of woman. She makes no apologies for who she is, her journey, and she simply gets to the point. After meeting Naomi a few years ago, I quickly learned she is a woman with a purpose on a mission for God. As sisters in Christ, we have walked in the zone of discomfort and made our share of mistakes, but it's in those difficult times we have shared our greatest victories.

Unapologetically Here is not just the title of a book, it is a call to action. It's time to stop apologizing to people who add little value to your life. Confront what is buried in your past so that you may defeat it. Surround yourself with like-minded visionaries who will challenge you and hold you accountable. In this book, Naomi has challenged us to show up and be ready for what God has in store.

Are you ready? YES, you are!

Malai R. Pressley, Ed.S.
Educator, Founder of Briteside™,
Columbia, SC

ABOUT THE AUTHOR

Naomi P. Washington is the Founder and CEO of NewPlaceWithin, LLC. NewPlaceWithin inspires, motivates, and encourages others to live their purpose unapologetically. Naomi became passionate about writing at a young age and was encouraged in March of 2011 to begin a blog. Cathartic blogging for her quickly became fortifying for others. In January 2016 her designed purpose of using words to engage and strengthen others went from a blog to a business.

Naomi is driven by her personal story of survival and has a passion for helping others to live unapologetically on purpose. Naomi started her company after meeting many women who, like her, struggled with today's demanding lifestyle and expectations. Naomi permitted herself to live her own life unapologetically and through consulting, speaking, and writing Naomi lives boldly, deliberately, and unapologetically in her purpose on purpose. Naomi P Washington is a consultant committed to empowering individuals using a no-nonsense approach while leveraging her knowledge, skills, and experiences to help them take charge of their lives. Naomi inspires their shift from position to purpose while maximizing the gifts and skills to create their ideal life.

Naomi's innate sense of compassion is what lead her to pursue a career in Social Work. Naomi holds a Bachelor of Arts degree in Social Work from Columbia College in Columbia South Carolina and a Masters of Arts degree in Human Services, Marriage and Family Counseling from Liberty University in Lynchburg Virginia. Naomi is an established professional in the field of social work and human services. She has nearly ten years of experience in the State of South Carolina and other Non-Profit and Educational organizations in South Carolina. While she passionately stands in her purpose, she can also be found loving, laughing, and living in her role as mother, wife, sister, daughter, and friend. She spends her time in Columbia, SC with her husband Kevin, daughters Sauntavia and Kearyn, and son Nathan. She enjoys reading, Pinterest"ing" for crafts or recipes, and curling up under her favorite blue comforter with a Chai Tea Latte!

Contact Naomi P Washington
www.NaomiPWashington.com
Facebook: www.Facebook.com/NaomiPWashington
Twitter: @NPWashington

www.ingramcontent.com/pod-product-compliance
Lightning Source LLC
Chambersburg PA
CBHW070531100426
42743CB00010B/2042